W9-DJE-978

THE
ANALYTIC
TRADITION
IN
PHILOSOPHY
BACKGROUND
AND
ISSUES

THE
ANALYTIC
TRADITION
IN
PHILOSOPHY
BACKGROUND
AND
ISSUES

MICHAEL CORRADO
Ohio University

AMERICAN LIBRARY ASSOCIATION
Chicago 1975

Library of Congress Cataloging in Publication Data

Corrado, Michael, 1940–
    The analytic tradition in philosophy.

    Bibliography: p.
    1. Analysis (Philosophy) I. Title.
B808.5.C64   149'.94   75–9801
ISBN O–8389–0190–5
ISBN 0–8389–0204–9 pbk.

to Gail

Contents

Acknowledgments

Readers who are acquainted with the work of Roderick Chisholm will see that I have relied heavily on it. That is not to say, of course, that I have agreed with everything I have understood him to say; and I am confident that he would not agree with everything I have said here. Still, I have used much that I learned from him, especially in chapters 3, 4, and 6; and I wish to acknowledge here an indebtedness that is much too general to be conveyed by footnotes. I want also to express my gratitude to Professor Henry Johnstone for his kindness and encouragement, and for his helpful comments about the text.

Of the many colleagues at both Ohio University and the Pennsylvania State University from whom I have learned much about what analytic philosophy is, and about what it is not, I must mention in particular Gene Blocker, Richard Butrick, Alan Goldman, David Lincicome, Robert Price, Warren Ruchti, Elizabeth Smith, Robert Trevas, Carl Vaught, Robert Wieman, and especially David Stewart, without whose help this book would not have been possible. At several points I have made use of insights that came from James Fulton of Wichita State University. Finally, for the most careful readings of the manuscript and the most encouraging remarks, I am grateful to two philosophers in my family: my wife, to whom I have dedicated the book, and my brother, Jack Corrado.

My thanks to the *Journal of Philosophy* and to Roderick Chisholm for permission to reprint part of Professor Chisholm's "Problem of Empiricism" (1948) in chapter 3; and to Simon and Schuster and to George Allen and Unwin for permission to quote from Bertrand Russell's *My Philosophical Development* in chapters 3 and 4.

The Central Fund for Research of the College of Liberal Arts at Penn State provided funds for typing and clerical work.

This discussion of analytic philosophy is intended to be complemented by the description of contemporary European philosophy in David Stewart and Algis Mickunas, *Exploring Phenomenology* (Chicago: American Library Association, 1974).

Introduction

The analytic tradition is an important one in recent philosophy. Nearly all the important philosophical work that goes on in the English-speaking countries, for example, is in the analytic tradition. Nevertheless, it is notoriously difficult to draw the boundaries of analytic philosophy, and it is important to realize that the tradition is just that: a tradition. There is no single method, nor any set of problems that can be called distinctively analytic, nor is there any single man around whose work analytic philosophy has been built. Even so, philosophers do know how to apply the term, and they do know, for the most part, what is to count as analytic philosophy and what is not. In this Introduction, before setting out the plan of the book, I will try to explain just what analytic philosophy, in this very broad sense, is.

WHAT IS ANALYTIC PHILOSOPHY?

First of all, we can attempt a general characterization of the work of philosophers. Among the tasks that fall to philosophy is the task of defining the subject matter of other areas of study. The proper subject matter of psychology, physics, biology, history, and mathematics is the subject of philosophical discussion, but there is no other discipline that decides for philosophy what the subject matter of philosophy is. *What is it that psychology does?* is not a psychological question, and *What is it that physics does?* is not a question for physics to answer. Of course the psychologist or the physicist may deal with these questions. The point is that if he does he is engaging in philosophy, and not in psychology or physics. But *What is the subject matter of philosophy? is* a philosophical question. Consequently some writers, in trying to say what philosophy is, have said something like this: It is the field in which investigators are entitled by their official capacity to ask, What am I doing?

However appealing that description of philosophy and philosophers might be, it does little to enlighten the uninitiated reader about what other sorts of questions philosophers deal with. And it seems to me that it is more important to introduce the new reader to the problems that have puzzled philosophers than to say to him just what philosophy is. I would even be tempted, sometimes, to say that too great a concern about just what philosophy is can have a paralyzing effect on philosophical investigation.

So, what is it that philosophers investigate? G. E. Moore said that the most important job of a philosopher is to list all the sorts of things that there are in the universe. That is certainly one of the jobs that philosophers have undertaken. What Moore was asking for was not an inventory of each table, chair, horse, person, and telephone that is to be found. He meant, rather, something like this: It is the job of the philosopher to determine whether we must suppose that there are material objects in the universe, and whether we must suppose that there are minds in addition to material objects (or are human beings *just* material objects, or are they neither material objects nor material objects *with* minds, but something else entirely?), and must we concede that properties—like redness—exist? And, even if there are both things and properties, must we also recognize the existence of facts that unite thing and property? Are there that many kinds of things in the universe, or are there just material objects, as the materialist supposes?

Other questions philosophers have occupied themselves with are: What is knowledge? How is it possible to know things about the world outside us? How is it possible to know laws of science? What are persons? What are free actions? What actions are right actions, and what ends are worth striving for? And, as I have already indicated, philosophers consider such questions as: What is the subject matter of psychology? Is it mental events or just behavior? What is the difference between mental events and behavior? How is the subject matter of biology to be distinguished from the subject matter of physics? Are mathematical truths just logical truths?

But this list is far from containing every question, or even every sort of question, to which philosophers have addressed themselves. Someone has remarked that the only way to discover what questions belong to philosophy is to study what questions philosophers have undertaken to answer. But even that is not quite right; some philosophers have tried to answer questions of psychology and thought mistakenly that they were doing philosophy. Nevertheless, we may have to settle for the general agreement of philosophers concerning what the questions of philosophy are; that may be the best we can do. If there is any characteristic that belongs to all and to only philosophical questions, I don't know what it is. If we cannot say what philosophy is, we are no better off trying to say what a philosophical question is. We will have to settle for the list, as deficient as it is.

Now as bad as things are for saying what philosophy is, and what a philosophical question is, things are even worse for trying to say what analytic philosophy is. In this case I cannot even point to a common set of problems that are the subject matter for analytic philosophy and for no other philosophical tradition. It is certainly not the questions they deal with that sets analytic philosophers apart.

What complicates the problem here is that I am using the term *analytic* to cover the work of philosophers who would deny being analysts in any strict sense. There is no choice; there is no other word in common usage that refers to what is very definitely a philosophical tradition, but one so loosely structured that it is impossible to find any characteristic that applies to all and only philosophers in that tradition. There is not even a distinctive method that can be singled out as analytic. Many of the methods in use by analytic philosophers today seem to have been used by Franz Brentano, for example; Brentano was not an analyst. He was the teacher of Edmund Husserl, who founded the phenomenological school—a school lying outside the analytic tradition. And some of the methods of the earlier analysts are rejected by later analysts.

Nevertheless, when analysis is opposed to other important contemporary traditions—phenomenology, for example—philosophers know pretty well who is to count as an analyst and who is not. The term *analyst* applies, in this very loose sense, to the majority of the important philosophers in the English-speaking countries, and in Scandinavia. They are philosophers who have been influenced by Bertrand Russell and G. E. Moore, Ludwig Wittgenstein, the logical positivists, especially Rudolf Carnap, and American pragmatists, especially C. I. Lewis, or else they have been influenced by men who were influenced by those philosophers. There is no body of doctrine that all analysts have in common, nor any method that they share. There is a pretty general interest among analysts in logic and in formal structures, but that interest is by no means universal. Analytic philosophers are sometimes called linguistic philosophers. In one sense they are. They make use of language in trying to discover things about the world, but in that sense all philosophers are linguistic philosophers. In another popular sense of linguistic philosopher—a student of linguistic expressions and their interrelations only—we may say: There was a time when some analytic philosophers would have called themselves linguistic philosophers, but now none would. Some analysts have stressed the importance of creating an ideal language in which everything could be said, but by means of which we could not be led into philosophical mistakes. But not all analysts have believed in the possibility of the ideal language; some have argued that ordinary language is already perfect for its purpose. Perhaps the most we can say is this: Analytic philosophy is what is done by those philosophers who were taught—directly or indirectly—by the men listed earlier in this paragraph. That gives an idea, at best a rough one, of who the analytic philosophers are. But to say that analytic philosophy is the philosophy they do is not very revealing.

But even if it is not very revealing, it is the best I can do in one or two lines. For a better answer, the only alternative is to try to find out just how different analytic philosophers have proceeded. And that is the point of the book, to show what analytic philosophy is, by showing what it is that analytic philosophers have done. Let us talk, therefore, about the plan of the book.

THE PLAN OF THE BOOK

The book is divided into two parts. The first part provides the general background; the second part deals with problems or areas that have received special attention from analytic philosophers. In many books it makes no difference where the reader starts. In this book none of the chapters in part 2 presupposes any of the others, but each of them presupposes part 1. The reader who has had little previous exposure to philosophy had better read part 1 first. The purpose of part 1 is to sketch the history of analytic philosophy from its beginning around the turn of the century until about 1930, to sketch it in such a way that the problems treated in part 2 can be put into their proper perspective and context. The reader is warned against supposing that part 1 is simple history; it is abbreviated history, with a purpose—to make the discussion in part 2 intelligible.

Chapter 1 is devoted to developments in logic and metaphysics; the analysis it considers is the sort done by the logical atomists. There was considerable concern at that time with the idea that the structure of language somehow reflected the structure of the world. The job of the analyst was very generally considered to be the job of finding the *true* but perhaps hidden structure of propositions which underlay their possibly misleading grammatical structure. The true structure of "The average man is 5' 11" tall" cannot be subject-predicate, for example; if it were, we would have to suppose that the subject—the average man—must somehow exist for the sentence to be true. It is up to the analyst to show the true form of the proposition. Of course the propositions the atomists were concerned with were not about the average man, but about philosophically more interesting topics.

Chapter 2 is about knowledge and meaning. It traces developments in epistemology—the study of knowledge—from the atomists up through the logical positivists. The positivists saw the function of the philosopher much the same as the atomists had, with this exception: the positivist was not concerned to learn from the structure of language anything about what *really* exists in the world. The positivist denied the meaningfulness of questions about what there is—questions about metaphysics. That is what positivism has always meant, a denial of the possibility of doing metaphysics. What distinguished the logical positivists from earlier positivists is that they found metaphysical assertions—there is a God, there is no afterlife, there are minds, there are no minds—not only impossible to support; they found them meaningless. To help them keep the meaningful sentences clear of the meaningless ones, they had something called the verifiability criterion. The job of the analyst was to determine which sentences were meaningful, and to show that if we understand correctly the structure of language, philosophical problems do not arise. The problem of perception—what is the relationship between my experience and the things that I experience—is easily solved when we realize that statements about the things we experience—tables, chairs, other persons—are really just constructions out of statements about experience; at least that is the solution that seemed acceptable at that time.

All the chapters in part 2 are devoted to more recent work done by analytic philosophers in specific areas. There are four chapters. Chapter 3 is concerned with the theory of knowledge, chapter 4 with the philosophy of mind, chapter 5 with ethical philosophy, and chapter 6 with the philosophy of logic. Each of the chapters begins with a position that was pretty widely accepted in the early years of analysis, or that was somehow characteristic of or called for by either atomism or positivism. The philosophy of perception developed in chapter 2 is called phenomenalism; that is where our study of knowledge begins in chapter 3. The philosophy of mind called for by both atomism and positivism seems to have been behaviorism—in a way, behaviorism follows from the verifiability criterion of meaning; chapter 4 begins with behaviorism. Moore's ethical theory must have been congenial to atomists; in any case emotivism was congenial to the positivists; our look at ethics in chapter 5 begins with Moore's theory and moves quickly to emotivism. The position we start with in each of those three chapters turns out to be untenable; after showing why, more plausible theories are discussed. The structure of the sixth chapter is not so simple. The sixth chapter is not only a reworking of the discussion that has taken place concerning certain problems in the philosophy of logic, it is also a summing up. In a way, there were problems of the philosophy of logic being worked out in each of the other chapters; in chapter 6 we are in a position to say something about the philosophy of logic because of what we have learned in the other chapters. The views of the atomists were in large part views about the philosophy of logic; in chapter 6, having discussed much of the recent work done in analytic philosophy, I take the opportunity to discuss the fate of those views.

I have tried hard to make the book a unified discussion of analytic philosophy; perhaps it is not necessary to point out that some distortion has necessarily taken place. I am not too concerned about that. The book was never intended as a bible, but rather as a handbook from which the interested reader might find his way into the literature. I hope it will serve that purpose.

PART 1

THE
BACKGROUND

CHAPTER 1

LOGIC
AND
METAPHYSICS

The project in these first two chapters will be to retrace the course of analytic philosophy through the first decades of this century. You are more apt, in the literature of this philosophical tradition, to come upon careful discussion of a single point than to come upon a completed system of any kind. Unhappily it is often impossible to learn from such a discussion what the context was in which that discussion arose or what the point of the discussion is. We must bring to such discussions, including those in the later chapters of this book, an understanding of their context and an idea of the general direction in which they will go. These two preliminary chapters, therefore, will try to convey a sense of the context and direction of the discussions of analytic philosophers. Those things are best conveyed by examining the goals and methods of the founders of this type of philosophy, the problems they took to be their own, the success they had in solving those problems, and their failures. The first two chapters are devoted to this examination. Then, after we have established a direction, we can take up the more restricted studies of more recent philosophers.

PRINCIPIA MATHEMATICA

Of all the philosophical problems that faced the early analysts it would be most profitable to begin with the one that was attacked by Bertrand Russell and Alfred North Whitehead in *Principia Mathematica*: How is it that true mathematical propositions cannot, under any circumstances, be false?[1]

Many of the propositions we know to be true could have been false under different circumstances. The proposition that Abraham Lincoln was president in 1862 is true. Yet it might have been false. Suppose events had gone otherwise; suppose Lincoln had had to withdraw before the 1860 elections for reasons of health. A world in which events followed that course, rather than the course they did follow, is certainly possible. But in what world, under what circumstances, could 2 plus 2 equal 5? Many true propositions, like the one about Lincoln, just happen to be true. They could have been false. But the propositions of mathematics do not just happen to be true; if they are true at all they are necessarily true and cannot be false. Under the right circumstances men could have been one-legged, it would seem, but there is no set of circumstances under which two and two is not four, or in which three is greater than five.

This simple fact about mathematics has always disturbed philosophers, who have tried to explain it in various ways. Two of these attempts deserve our consideration—one because it represents an approach to philosophy rejected by analytic philosophers, and the other because it laid the foundation for so much later discussion.

The first way is this:

> *"Two plus two equals four" does not really say anything about the world; nor does any mathematical truth. What they do tell us about is the structure of the mind. The propositions of mathematics are really propositions about the way in which men must think. Whoever thinks "two plus two" cannot help but think "four." Naturally we cannot*

---

1. Bertrand Russell and Alfred North Whitehead, *Principia Mathematica* (Cambridge: Cambridge Univ. Pr., 1910–13), pp. v–viii.

*imagine a world in which the propositions of mathematics
are false; we cannot think in ways in which we cannot think.
Thus the apparent necessity of the laws of mathematics de-
rives from the fact that they describe ways in which men
must think, the human mind being what it is.*

This explanation of the necessity of the laws of mathematics,
which has been called a psychologistic explanation, is unsatisfactory. You will find a discussion of it in Bertrand Russell's
The Problems of Philosophy.[2] Although Russell attributes this
sort of explanation to Kant, what Russell is really arguing
against is every attempt to psychologize the laws of mathematics, to reduce the necessity of mathematical propositions in some
way to the compulsion of the so-called laws of thought. Psychologism must fail to account for the necessity of mathematical
propositions. To see why, you need only consider whether the
structure of the mind could be different. If it could, then according to psychologism the laws of mathematics could be different; but the laws of mathematics could not be different. So
suppose the structure of the mind could not be different. This
solves the problem of the necessity of the propositions of mathematics, but leaves us with another puzzle. Why is it that the
structure of the mind could not be different? We have only
pushed the problem back a step. Either way, the psychologistic
explanation fails as an explanation.

A more promising sort of solution is this one:

*The propositions of mathematics are true in virtue of the
meanings of the words involved in those propositions. All
mathematics can be reduced to arithmetic; and arithmetic
can, by means of logic and definitions, be reduced to simple
logical truths. Mathematical propositions cannot be false,
just as "a is a" cannot be false. But just like "a is a," the
reason they cannot be false is that they do not say anything; they are trivial.*

This was, we shall see, Russell's way. The thesis that all mathematics can be reduced to logic is called the logistic thesis; the
position is called logicism. According to logicism, the necessity
of "2 plus 2 is 4" lies in the meanings of the words; since "2"

2. Bertrand Russell, *The Problems of Philosophy* (London: Oxford
Univ. Pr., and New York: Henry Holt, 1912), pp. 127–41.

means the same as "1 plus 1" and "4" means the same as "1 plus 1 plus 1 plus 1," "2 plus 2 is 4" cannot be false simply because it does nothing more than state the identity "1 plus 1 plus 1 plus 1 is 1 plus 1 plus 1 plus 1." Russell collaborated with A. N. Whitehead in the attempt to work out the logistic explanation. As I have presented it here, after all, logicism is not yet an explanation; it is a suggestion for an explanation, or a program, or a pious hope, or a dogma. The explanation itself would consist in the demonstration that every truth of mathematics—or at least that every kind of truth of mathematics—could be reduced to logical truths by means of definitions.

Russell first sketched out the program in *The Principles of Mathematics*.[3] His work had been inspired, as he willingly admitted, by the work of the Italian school of mathematicians headed by Peano, which had succeeded in deriving all of arithmetic from a small set of premises, and later on by the work of the German mathematician and philosopher Frege, who had reduced certain mathematical ideas to logical notions. Both men had also developed a logical symbolism, which would free the mathematician from having to depend on his intuitive grasp of the logical terms. The logical symbolism could be manipulated only according to clearly defined procedures, and there was no room, as we shall see when we study the symbolism, to smuggle in unwarranted assumptions.[4] With these advances the prospects for the reduction of mathematics to logic seemed bright. Russell sketched in the various reductions rather informally in the *Principles*; it remained for the derivation of mathematics to be worked out in detail. It was this task that Russell and Whitehead undertook in *Principia Mathematica*.

They did not entirely succeed. It became apparent that the principles of logic and definitions would not suffice; certain other principles are needed, principles with an irreducibly mathematical flavor. For example, to guarantee that two different numbers cannot have the same successor, it is necessary to assume that there is an infinity of things in the universe; that

3. Bertrand Russell, *The Principles of Mathematics* (Cambridge: Cambridge Univ. Pr., 1903). In what follows we will discuss only a part of the logic to which mathematics was supposed to be reducible. The logic of the *Prinicipia Mathematica* was richer than what, for our purposes, it is necessary to develop.

4. For a discussion of the new logic and its symbolism, *see* chapter 6 of John Passmore's *Hundred Years of Philosophy* (New York: Basic Books, 1966), "New Developments in Logic."

assumption is called the axiom of infinity.[5] Such principles are not logical principles, and yet they are necessary for the derivation of mathematics. It seems that logicism will also fail as an account of the necessity of mathematical propositions.

But although the *Principia* was not successful in showing that the logistic thesis could be worked out, it had a tremendous impact on the philosophical world. Philosophical problems had notoriously resisted solution; Kant had called it a scandal. It sometimes seemed that philosophers continually went over the same ground, without solving a single problem. But all that was over with; here was an important step toward the solution of a philosophical problem. If the difficulties could be ironed out, the problem would be solved. Mathematical propositions cannot be false because they are not really about the world—they are really just complicated logical truths. Furthermore, if the difficulties could *not* be worked out, if some obstacle appeared which could not be overcome, that too would be an answer; the logistic thesis is false. In either case progress would be made.

Much of the credit for the progress that was made belonged to techniques made possible by the development of symbolic logic. These techniques are central to analytic philosophy, and we are interested in the *Principia* because of those techniques, and not because of any interest in the complex philosophy of mathematics, which lies outside the scope of this book. We will say no more about mathematics, therefore, and look instead to the technical developments of more general philosophical importance. We must begin with a look at the logic of the *Principia*.

THE NEW LOGIC

The principles of the new logic were fairly simple. Logic is an old study, but as a study it had not advanced for nearly two thousand years. Then in the fifty years or so preceding the publication of the *Principia*, things changed. Most notably, logic was given a symbolism which made possible proofs that relied not at all on the intuitions of the logician, eliminating a source of error and making possible calculations more extensive than had previously been possible. It was compressed into a system of axioms, making possible the consideration of a logical system as

5. *See* Bertrand Russell's *Introduction to Mathematical Philosophy* (New York and London: Allen & Unwin, 1919), chapter 13.

a whole, and, most important of all, it included, as the older logic had not, the logic of the relations things bore to one another. It is difficult to understand just what these last two achievements amount to without knowing something of the symbolism. Since the symbolism is rather easy to explain, it will be profitable to take the time to explain it.[6]

We need a symbolism for sentences. Depending on how much of the structure of the sentence we want to expose, we can symbolize a sentence like "Socrates is a man" with a single letter (usually "A" or "B" or "C," or some other capital letter from that part of the alphabet), or with separate symbols for the name "Socrates" and the predicate "is a man" (some appropriate lower case letter for the name, some capital for the predicate), put together in this way: "Ms," where "s" is the name, "M" the predicate. When we use predicates, it is possible to use variables instead of names; the variables come from the end of the alphabet, just as they do in algebra—"x," "y," "z." Where "F" is some predicate, we read "Fx" in this way: "x has property F," or simply "x is F." In addition to the predicates we need symbols for relations. In "Herbert loves Martha" the word "loves" is a relation-word, and we symbolize it by a capital letter. If "h" is "Herbert," "m" is "Martha," and "L" is "loves," the sentence is given by "hLm." And in general to say that x loves y we would write "xLy." Relations may hold between two things, or three things, or more. Betweenness, for example, is a relation of three things: "x is between y and z."

From such simple sentences as those symbolized by "A" and "B" and "Ms" and "Fx" and "hLm," we may form compounds and generalizations. The principles of logic are just principles governing this compounding and generalization. The particular compounds studied in the *Principia*, where "A" and "B" are sentences, were conjunctions:

$$\text{"A \& B" for "A and B,"}$$

disjunctions:

$$\text{"A v B" for "A or B,"}$$

negations:

$$\text{"-A" for "not A,"}$$

6. Conventions have changed some since 1915. The symbolism I present here is not exactly that of Russell-Whitehead, but it is very much like it and it is one that the reader is more likely to encounter.

and hypotheticals:

"A ⊃ B" for "if A then B,"
"A ≡ B" for "A if and only if B."

Here is some of the logic of conjunction. Suppose "F*a* & G*b*" is true; then "F*a*" is true. Suppose "F*a*" is true; suppose "G*b*" is true; then "F*a* & G*b*" is also true. The principle of double negation governs negation. Suppose "- - F*a*" is true; then "F*a*" is also true. For disjunction: suppose "F*a*" is true; then "F*a* v G*b*" is also true. For the hypothetical: suppose "F*a* ⊃ G*b*" and "F*a*" are both true; then "G*b*" is also true. What holds for "F*a*" and "G*b*" holds for any sentences whatever.

Generalizations of "F*a*" are sentences expressing the proposition that everything is F and the proposition that something is F:

"(*x*)(F*x*)" for "Everything is F,"
"(∃*x*)(F*x*)" for "Something is F."

In these sentences, "(*x*)" and "(∃*x*)" are called quantifiers. Again principles govern the relationship between particular and general sentences. Here are two of them: Suppose *a* is F; then something is F (suppose "F*a*" is true; then "(∃*x*)(F*x*)" is true). Suppose everything is F; then *a* is F (suppose "(*x*)(F*x*)" is true; then "F*a*" is also true).

These principles, and all of the principles of logic, can be derived from the axioms and rules given in part 1 of the *Principia*. It was from these axioms and rules that the whole of mathematics was to be derived.

Was this system of logic consistent or did it contain some sort of contradiction? Are the logical truths that can be derived in the system all the logical truths that there are, or are there logical truths that cannot be derived? Such questions were not taken up by Russell and Whitehead, but because their system was, in a manner of speaking, captured in a small number of axioms and rules, the problem of answering such questions became more manageable; it became the problem of discovering whether the axioms were consistent, and of showing that every logical truth must be derivable from the axioms. In the case of the elementary part of the *Principia*, the logic is consistent, and it is also complete; every logical truth is derivable in it. These answers were provided by later writers.

The older logic, sometimes called Aristotelian logic, had no way of dealing with what we have called relations. That logic was only able to handle propositions expressed by sentences of the form "*a* is F," propositions in which some property was attributed to a subject. According to Russell this was no mere oversight; it rested on the conviction that all propositions were, in some ultimate sense, of the subject-predicate form and not relational. Sentences that seemed to express propositions relating *a* and *b* (the sentence "*a* is longer than *b*" for example) really expressed propositions that attributed some property to *a* and some property to *b* (in our example, that *a* is of such and such a length and that *b* is of such and such a length). There would be no need for sentences of a relational form like "*xRy*" or "*xTy,z*," but only for those, like "F*x*," which attributed some property to an individual. About this conviction two things can be said. In the first place, it is false. The old logic, without relations, was never able to capture the structure of mathematical arguments. It is not difficult to show that not all propositions can be reduced to subject-predicate propositions. The reduction suggested above—"*a* is longer than *b*" to "*a* is of such and such a length and *b* is of such and such a length"—does not work unless we can add that the first length is longer than the second, and that fact seems to be irreducibly relational.

Second, this conviction has led, all by itself, to some of the stranger speculative philosophies of the eighteenth and nineteenth centuries, if Russell is right. Monism, for example, the position that there is really only one thing (and that you and I are part of it) follows immediately, "since the fact that there were several substances (if it were a fact) would not have the requisite form;"[7] i.e., it would be relational and not subject-predicate. Russell felt that monism was sufficiently refuted by the proof that propositions like the proposition that *a* is longer than *b* are relational, for if they are relational the terms of such relations must be two things, and not one. Since some such propositions are true there is more than one thing, and monism is false; it cannot account for the fact that some tables are longer than others, for example.

Monism was one of the tenets of the philosophical idealism that dominated British philosophy at the end of the nineteenth century. British idealism is seen by some historians as an aberration in the philosophical history of a people whose dominant tendencies in philosophy have always been either empiricist or common sense. The idealists in Britain were followers of either

---

7. Bertrand Russell, "Logical Atomism," in *Logical Positivism*, ed. by Alfred J. Ayer (New York: Free Pr., 1959), p. 39.

Kant or Hegel. Russell tells us that "Hegelians had all kinds of arguments to prove this or that not 'real'. Number, space, time, matter, were all professedly convicted of being self-contradictory. Nothing was real, so we were assured, except the Absolute [hence the monism]."[8] An equally important tenet of idealism was this one: Only what is apprehended by a mind can exist, or, in other words, everything that exists depends for its existence on some mind; there is nothing which is independent of all minds. Russell began his career as an idealist, but in the 1890s under the influence of his friend, G. E. Moore, he repudiated that doctrine. The two men are largely responsible for leading British philosophy away from idealism. Their influence was so complete that the English-speaking world has today few proponents of that philosophy.

With the logic of relations, symbolic logic was immensely more powerful than Aristotelian logic had been. With names, predicates, and relation-words we can say a great deal more about the structure of the world than the old logic could say with just names and predicates. As we have seen, the old logic could not handle something as simple as that this object is longer than that. Could the new logic say everything that had to be said? Were there sufficient features in the logic to reflect the features of the world, or were there features the new logic didn't capture just as the old had not captured relations? The conviction that the logic of the *Principia* did reflect the structure of the world guided analytic philosophy in its early years.

ATOMISM

What does it mean to say that a logic reflects the world? Let's start from the other direction. We've already seen a way in which a logic did not reflect the world—in the older logic there was no way to express the proposition that objects are related in certain ways. In general, Russell claimed, the logic of ordinary grammar did not reflect reality accurately. If we started with the categories of our language and inferred from them something about the structure of the world, we were very likely to be mistaken in our inference. As in the case of monism, which

8. Bertrand Russell, *My Philosophical Development* (London: Allen & Unwin, 1959), p. 62. On British idealism, *see* Passmore's *Hundred Years of Philosophy*, chapter 3.

derived support from the fact that in the Indo-European languages sentences can often be put into subject-predicate form, outrageous philosophical positions are often based on such mistaken inferences. In the essay "Logical Atomism," Russell wrote:

> The influence of language on philosophy has, I believe, been profound and almost unrecognized. If we are not to be misled by this influence, it is necessary to become conscious of it, and to ask ourselves deliberately how far it is legitimate. The subject-predicate logic, with the substance-attribute metaphysic, are a case in point. It is doubtful whether either would have been invented by people speaking a non-Aryan language. . . . As language grows more abstract, a new set of entities come into philosophy, namely, those represented by abstract words—the universals. I do not wish to maintain that there are no universals, but certainly there are many abstract words that do not stand for single universals—e.g., triangularity and rationality. In these respects language misleads us both by its vocabulary and by its syntax. We must be on our guard in both respects if our logic is not to lead us to a false metaphysic.[9]

Suppose a sentence expresses the proposition that certain things are arranged in a certain way. If the grammatical form of the sentence does not reflect accurately that arrangement, then the form is not correct. The form of a sentence is correct when to every element in the arrangement there corresponds a name in the sentence, and the structure of the arrangement is mirrored in the structure of the arrangement of the names in the sentence. A language in which only the correct form is possible for a sentence might be called an "ideal language." From a description of the world in such an ideal language we would not be able to draw any of the paradoxical conclusions of which the older philosophers were so fond. After sketching such a language, Russell says:

> The purpose of the foregoing discussion of an ideal logical language (which would of course be wholly useless for daily life) is two-fold: first, to prevent inferences from the nature of language to the nature of the world which are fallacious because they depend upon the logical defects of language; secondly, to suggest, by inquiring what logic requires of a language which is to avoid contradiction, what sort of structure we may reasonably suppose the world to have.[10]

9. Russell, "Logical Atomism," p. 38.
10. Ibid., p. 45.

Some philosophers were convinced that their investigations would show that the world is made up of atomic facts, and they were called, accordingly, logical atomists. Besides Russell the group included a number of well-known philosophers (not, interestingly, either Whitehead or Moore); the best known of all was Russell's student and friend, Ludwig Wittgenstein.[11] It was clear to Wittgenstein that the world is a collection of facts, and that all these facts, and all possible facts, are atomic. That means that no fact contains another fact as a part; there are no facts about facts. All facts are atomic, and they are all independent of one another. While sentences might be complex, that is not to be taken to mean that there are complex facts; there are none.

To such a world the logic of the *Principia* is adequate. There are individuals in the world; correspondingly, there is a category of names in the language. Where there are combinations of individuals, called "facts," in the world, there are combinations of names, called sentences, in the language. A sentence *pictures* a fact; a sentence pictures a fact when the structure of the names in the sentence corresponds to the structure of the named individuals in the fact.

It is difficult to see precisely what is wanted here. The atomists themselves were not agreed about what this relation of "picturing," that holds between language and the world, is supposed to be. One possibility might be this. The linguistic relationship of being located on either side of "is next to" might correspond to the relationship objects bear to one another when they are next to each other; and so if "*a*" is the name of the object *a* and "*b*" is the name of the object *b*, then "*a* is next to *b*" would picture the fact that *a* is next to *b*. But it has also been suggested that in the ideal language the fact that *a* is next to *b* might be pictured simply by placing the name "*a*" next to the name "*b*"; and it has also been suggested that the fact in question involves not only *a* and *b*, but also nextness, and that the fact consists in the arrangement of these three things.

But about one thing there was pretty general agreement. To the logical connectives themselves—"and," "or," "if—then," and so on—nothing corresponds in reality. To say that "A & B" is true is not to say that there is in reality the fact that A, and there

---

11. A good discussion of atomism and the atomists is to be found in J. O. Urmson's *Philosophical Analysis* (Oxford: Clarendon Pr., 1956), pp. 1–98.

is in reality the fact that B, and there is yet another fact, namely that both facts occur. This last clause adds nothing. To say that "A & B" is true is just to say that there is in reality the fact that A, and that there is in reality the fact that B; nothing more. Conjunction, like disjunction and implication, is not a feature of the world but only of language. There are no conjunctive or disjunctive or conditional facts, but only atomic ones. Wittgenstein tried to show that even sentences like "$(x)(Fx)$"—"Everything is F"—correspond to atomic facts. Here is the general idea: If a, b, and c were all the individuals in the world, "$(x)(Fx)$" would correspond to the atomic facts that a is F, that b is F, and that c is F. The whole of this rather thin theory of meaning is called the picture theory of meaning; it was developed by Wittgenstein in his *Tractatus Logico-Philosophicus*.[12]

There are some obvious objections to the atomists' disconnected world, at least there seem to be. Facts seem to be related in different ways; they are not all independent. One may cause another, as smoking may bring about cancer. One fact may include another as a piece of knowledge. For example, the fact that Dante despised Boniface seems to be part of the fact that Boccaccio knew that Dante despised Boniface. Smoking causing the disease and Boccaccio knowing what he did about Dante seem to be complex facts. But according to atomism there are no such complex facts. We need no symbols for "causes" and "knows that," but only the logical connectives of the *Principia*. Is the atomist simply mistaken about this? Is the language of the *Principia* simply inadequate to describe the world as it really is?

The hope was that the philosopher could show that the language of the *Principia* was adequate to describe the world by coming up with the correct analyses of causal sentences, knowledge sentences, and other troublesome sorts of sentences; that these analyses would show what the correct logical form of such sentences are; and that in those analyses the analysans would consist of atomic sentences connected by "and," "or," "not," "if—then," and "if and only if." If this could be done, then it would have been demonstrated that there are no connections between facts which have to find expression in logic. There would not have to be, in the language, expressions for cause and knowledge and desire and belief and might-have-beens, because there would

12. Ludwig Wittgenstein, *Tractatus Logico-Philosophicus*, trans. by C. K. Ogden (London: Kegan Paul; New York: Harcourt, 1922); new trans. by D. F. Pears and B. F. McGuinness, 1961.

be nothing in reality for them to express. Anyone who believes a proposition about cause or desire really just believes that certain atomic states of affairs are facts, and that certain others are not.

The project then is to show that every complex sentence is equivalent to some sentence in which the atomic parts are connected only by the logical connectives of the *Principia*. If the project succeeded, then atomism would be vindicated. If atomism were vindicated, then the problem of explaining necessary connections between facts would be dissolved; there would be no such connections, mathematical, causal, or of any other kind. Precisely what had stood in the way of an older British empiricism was its inability to explain such connections; thus the vindication of atomism would serve the purposes of empiricism as well. The claim that this project could be carried out was called the thesis of *truth-functionality.*

TRUTH-FUNCTIONALITY

If there are no connections between the atomic facts, how do we account for what seem to be necessary connections? Consider these three atomic facts: My car is larger than my typewriter; my typewriter is larger than my pen; and my car is larger than my pen. These three facts seem not only to be related, but to be necessarily related. If the first and second are facts, then the third cannot fail to be a fact; if the first were a fact and the third were not, then the second could not be a fact. More precisely, it seems to be necessarily the case that if the first and second are facts then the third must also be, and that if the first is a fact and the third is not, then the second likewise is not. Is this not a case of necessary connection?

We have already seen that the *Principia Mathematica* is an extended attempt to analyze such truths as "if a is greater than b and b is greater than c then a is greater than c" in such a way that it can be seen that they are just logical truths, and that the necessity of such truths is just logical necessity. But how are we to explain logical necessity, if we are to maintain that there are no connections between facts?

Wittgenstein explained it this way in the *Tractatus*:[13] Logical necessity is empty. It is logically necessary that it is either raining or not raining; "$p \lor -p$" is logically necessary, for any sen-

---

13. *See* section 5 of the *Tractatus.*

tence "*p*." But that it is either raining or not raining tells us nothing about the world; no information about the state of the weather is conveyed. It is precisely because of this lack of information, because "it is raining or not raining" rules out no state of affairs, that such sentences are logically necessary. Sentences that are logically true are called tautologies. Which sentences are tautologies can be determined from the meanings of the logical connectives.

The meanings of the connectives are given by means of truth-tables, in this way:

A	B	A & B	-A	A v B	A ⊃ B	A ≡ B
T	T	T	F	T	T	T
T	F	F	F	T	F	F
F	T	F	T	T	T	F
F	F	F	T	F	T	T

The tables give the truth conditions under which the compound sentences are true or false. Reading "true" for "T" and "false" for "F," we can determine that when "A" and "B" are both true (the first line across) then "A & B" is true, "-A" is false, "A v B" is true, "A ⊃ B" is true, and "A ≡ B" is true. The other lines give the truth values of the compounds when "A" is true and "B" is false, when "A" is false and "B" is true, and when both are false. The necessary truth of the tautologies follows from these meanings, as we can see if we work out a truth table for "A v -A":

A	B	A v -A
T	T	T
T	F	T
F	T	T
F	F	T

"A" may be either true or false; in either case at least one of "A" and "-A" will turn out to be true: if "A" is true, then "A" is true, naturally, and if "A" is false, then "-A" is true. But that means that at least one of the disjuncts in "A v -A" must be true; and as we know from the truth table for "v," that means that "A v -A" will turn out to be true no matter what truth value is assigned to "A." That is why this sentence is a tautology. The same holds true for other logical truths like "A ⊃ A," "-(A & -A),'' "A ⊃ (B ⊃ A)," and "(A & (A ⊃ B)) ⊃ B."

The necessity of tautologies does not depend on relations between facts, then, but merely on the meanings we give to the connectives. Since there are no connections between events, all necessity, and not just mathematical necessity, must in the end be based on logical necessity. The job here for the analyst is to show how the necessary truths

> Bachelors are unmarried
> Every event has a cause
> What is red all over is not blue all over

can be analyzed into tautologies, just as Russell attempted to analyze the necessary truth that

> Two and two are four.

The connectives "and," "not," "or," "if—then," "if and only if," are called truth-functional because the truth value of any sentence made up only of atomic sentences and these connectives is fully determined by the truth values of the atomic parts. Whoever knows the truth value of "A," "B," and "C" can determine the truth value of "A v (B & C)," for example. The same is not true for all connectives. "Because" connects sentences, but it is not truth-functional; we may observe that a certain man is running, and we may observe that he is fat—but we cannot conclude just from that what the truth value of "He is running because he is fat" is. The truth value of "A because B" cannot be determined just from the truth value of "A" and the truth value of "B." That means that "because" is not a truth-functional connective.

The thesis of truth-functionality, then, is the thesis that all sentences can be translated into sentences whose only connectives are truth-functional, connectives whose meaning can be given on a truth table. The attempt to analyze causal sentences and knowledge sentences into truth-functions of atomic sentences is an attempt to work out the thesis of truth-functionality, and, as we have seen, if the thesis of truth-functionality can be defended, then so can atomism, and so can the claim that the language of the *Principia Mathematica* is adequate to the structure of the world.

THE THEORY OF
DESCRIPTIONS

The question of the adequacy of the language of the *Principia* arose as a result of the observation that another language would be inadequate—a language without relations. Yet our ordinary language had tempted philosophers into thinking we could get by with such a language. It was only careful attention to forms that had enabled Russell to see that such a language could not reflect the structure of the world—that we could not get by with just the subject-predicate form.

Russell and Wittgenstein believed that ordinary language is full of such snares for unwary philosophers. Wittgenstein wrote in the *Tractatus*:

> Most of the propositions and questions to be found in philosophical works are not false, but nonsensical. Consequently, we cannot give any answer to questions of this kind, but can only establish that they are non-sensical. Most of the propositions and questions of the philosophers arise from our failure to understand the logic of our language. . . . It was Russell who performed the service of showing that the apparent logical form of a proposition need not be its real one.[14]

Here is another way in which the apparent form of a proposition may lead us astray (and it is probably just this problem that Wittgenstein has in mind when he speaks of Russell's service): The sentence

Centaurs don't exist

seems to express a proposition of subject-predicate form. Yet if it is of subject-predicate form, it is not about anything; there is nothing for the subject term "centaurs" to refer to, since there are no centaurs, and consequently the proposition, which would be about centaurs if there were any, is not about anything. And since it is not about anything, it is without meaning, and so meaningless.

Despite the air of hocus-pocus about it, the problem is not so easily dispelled. What makes it so difficult is that any solution must also work for sentences like

The present king of France is bald,

whose subject term does not refer to anything since there is not presently any king of France. The solution Russell finally arrived at in his theory of descriptions was hailed as a paradigm of philosophy; it was one of the clearest examples of how the new methods were to be used to clear up old problems. But

14. Wittgenstein, *Tractatus* (1961), p. 37.

Russell entertained other solutions before he arrived at that one, and before we discuss the theory of descriptions we must take a longer look at the problem and some of the other solutions that were considered.

Here, then, is the problem to be met: If a sentence is of subject-predicate form, then the individual referred to by the subject term is part of the meaning of the sentence; it is what the sentence is about. Now consider sentences like

> Centaurs do not exist.
> The present king of France is bald.

If these sentences are of subject-predicate form, and what I have said about sentences of subject-predicate form is true, then they must be about whatever it is that "centaurs" and "the present king of France" refer to. But then they are about nothing, because those singular terms refer to nothing. Since those terms lack a meaning, the sentences lack meaning.

But they don't lack meaning; one of them is in fact true, and both are meaningful. How are we to deal with this problem? The first solution Russell tried he borrowed from the philosopher Alexius Meinong.[15] Meinong argued that it is a mistake to suppose that there aren't any centaurs or that there isn't any present king of France. Not that there are any *existent* centaurs; everyone knows there are no existent centaurs. And there is no existent king of France. What we must allow, according to Meinong, is that there are centaurs of another sort than existent; what might be called merely possible centaurs. Possible centaurs are just like existent centaurs, except for one thing; they don't exist. Nevertheless there are such (nonexistent) things. They differ in the manner in which they are; they are not existing entities, they are possible entities. You must not take this to mean simply that there *could* be such things. According to Meinong, there *are* such things; they are in the realm of the possible. This realm of possible beings includes both the existent entities and those which are merely possible entities. Although Hamlet was not actual, there is a possible object Hamlet. There is no present king of France, but the idea of a present king of France is in no way inconsistent; so, although the king is not an existent object, he is a possible object.

---

15. For a discussion of Meinong's position, *see* the "Introduction," in *Realism and the Background of Phenomenology*, ed. by Roderick M. Chisholm (Glencoe, Ill.: Free Pr., 1960), pp. 4–12.

With such possible objects, we can preserve the simplicity of our theory of meaning. Sentences have a meaning only if every noun phrase occurring in them has a reference, and of course every name does have a reference, if not to an existent object, then to a possible object. The sentence

Centaurs do not exist

is about something; it is about all possible centaurs. It says about them that they don't exist. Similarly

Pegasus is a winged horse

is about the possible object Pegasus.

Some philosophers—Meinong's teacher Brentano was one—objected to the idea of possible objects on the ground that there could be no way to determine what made just one possible object.[16] Consider the possible object which is king of France. Is he alone, or are there other possible kings of France? What about the possible *bald* king of France and the possible *red-haired* king of France? Is either one identical with the possible king of France? How does one decide?

Whatever the merits of the idea of possible objects all by itself, as a solution to our problem it could not succeed. For as Meinong saw, a complete solution of this sort would require not only possible objects, but also *impossible* objects. How else could sentences like

Round squares do not exist

and

The largest prime number doesn't exist

be meaningful? If we are going to use Meinong's solution, then there must be some sort of (nonexistent) entities for the subject terms to refer to. But these entities are not possible objects; neither round squares nor the largest prime is possible. They must be impossible objects. The need for such impossible objects is the worst feature of Meinong's solution. Russell abandoned that solution; it offended against what he had called a "robust sense of reality."

It is important to notice that the problem we are confronted with arises in part because of a certain view about the way in

16. Brentano's objections are also voiced by W. V. O. Quine in "On What There Is," in *From a Logical Point of View* (Cambridge: Harvard Univ. Pr., 1953), p. 3ff.

which names have meaning, a view that was to be incorporated later into the atomist picture theory of meaning. The meaning of a name, or of any singular term, is the thing it refers to. Russell's theory of descriptions manages to salvage that view of meaning, and thus helps to pave the way for atomism. But before we get to the theory of descriptions, it will be interesting to examine an alternative to the picture theory of meaning, one that separates the idea of meaning from the idea of reference. It was the work of Gottlob Frege, one of the mathematicians who influenced Russell's work, and it offers a solution to the problem we are dealing with, the problem of nonbeing. Russell discussed it in his paper "On Denoting," although he never held the theory himself.

According to Frege,[17] linguistic expressions have meaning on two levels. There is, in the first place, the referent of the expression; the referent of "Athens" is the city of Athens. In addition to its referent, every expression has a sense; the sense of "Athens" is the concept that the word expresses. The concept is different from the city, but both are nonmental entities; neither the city nor the concept is an idea existing *in* someone's mind. When we learn to use a word, we grasp the concept it expresses, and we can do that without knowing whether or not the word refers to anything. In this way we can understand sentences about the king of France, even though France is not a monarchy. "The king of France" has a sense, or meaning, even though it has no reference.

Every linguistic expression has these two levels of meaning, according to Frege: While names express concepts and refer to objects, sentences express propositions and, if all the names they contain refer to something, refer to either truth or falsity. If some of the names do not refer, the sentences do not refer— they are neither true nor false—but still they are meaningful; they express propositions. "The king of France is bald" is meaningful, since each of the names has a meaning; but it would not be true or false, since one of the names—"the king of France"— has no reference. But Russell maintained that not only were such sentences meaningful, they could also have a truth value.

---

17. Frege's theory is set out in his "On Sense and Denotation," which can be found in *Readings in Philosophical Analysis*, ed. by Herbert Feigl and Wilfrid S. Sellars (New York: Appleton, 1949); Russell's "On Denoting" is reprinted in his *Logic and Knowledge* (London: Allen & Unwin, 1956).

The theory of descriptions solution to the problem of non-referring terms was consistent with a one-level theory of meaning like the picture theory, and it had as a consequence that every meaningful sentence had to be true or false.[18] The theory goes roughly like this: Sentences like "The king of France is bald" and "Centaurs do not exist" appeal to the pernicious tendency to assume that all propositions are of subject-predicate form—of the form "Fa," where "a" is "the king of France" or "centaurs," and "F" is "is bald" or "do not exist." So we set about looking for objects to correspond to the subject terms, and when we find none we presume either that the sentence is meaningless, or that there are more objects than just those that happen to exist, or else that some alternative theory of meaning would be preferable. The truth is that the true logical form of the propositions expressed by these sentences is more complicated than the simple subject-predicate form, and once we see what that form is, we will see that such sentences are meaningful.

"Centaurs do not exist" is the easiest. We have in the language of the *Principia* a way to say that there are things with property F:

$$(\exists x)Fx,$$

that is, there is an x such that x is F. Now to say that centaurs do not exist is just to say that there are no centaurs, or that it is false that there are centaurs. Letting "C" be "is a centaur":

$$-(\exists x)Cx,$$

it is not the case that there is an x such that x is a centaur. This sentence is not really about centaurs; it is rather about everything that exists, and it says about each such thing that it has not the property of being a centaur.

That much is easy to see. What is not so easy to see is how that treatment might be extended to "The king of France is bald." Russell's claim is that this sentence too expresses an existential proposition. It says, after all, all of the following things: That there is something with the property of being king of France; that there is only one such thing; and that that thing is bald. It says nothing else. Since none of the things that exist have all those properties in conjunction (in particular, none has the property of being king of France), the statement is false. But a false statement is meaningful, and so we have accom-

---

18. The theory of descriptions is first set out in "On Denoting."

plished our purpose—to show how such statements could be meaningful without giving up the picture theory and without adding possible and impossible objects to the things that there are. In symbols we read the sentence in this way, letting "K" be "is king of France" and "B" be "is bald":

$$(\exists x)(Kx \ \& \ (y)(Ky \supset y = x) \ \& \ Bx);$$

there is an x such that x is a king of France, and for all y, if y is a king of France then y is x, and x is bald. The second clause— "$(y)(Ky \supset y = x)$"—can be called the uniqueness clause, and insures that the definite article "the" is translated from the original sentence. Without that clause we would have a translation of "Some king of France is bald." This sentence too is false, but it is not the sentence we started out with.

We have found the true logical form of the claim that the king of France is bald, and nowhere in it is there a reference to the king of France; it is about the things that exist. If the only things that existed were the individuals a, b, and c, then the claim would amount to this: Either a is the one and only thing with the property of being king of France and is bald, or b is the one and only thing with the property of being king of France and is bald, or c is the one and only thing with the property of being king of France and is bald. Here we are not talking about the king of France, but about a, b, and c, and attributing to one of them certain properties, among them the property of being king of France. And if there is no king of France, if neither a, b, nor c has the property of being king of France, then the claim is false. It is false because it does not picture things arranged as they are, because it pictures a state of affairs, or sets of states of affairs, which are not facts. Since it is false, it is meaningful, just as we knew it should be. Thus Russell's theory of descriptions, which says that most apparent singular terms are to be replaced with predicates and quantifiers, seemed to make possible a fully developed one-level theory of meaning; it was Wittgenstein who developed it, as we have seen, in the picture theory of meaning.

SUGGESTIONS
FOR FURTHER READING

The names associated with the beginnings of analysis are first and foremost those of Bertrand Russell and G. E. Moore. Frege and Whitehead were known to the early analysts because of Russell's work, and the same is true of Wittgenstein, who published little at that time.

A fine nontechnical introduction to the mathematical work of Russell and Whitehead is Russell's *Introduction to Mathematical Philosophy* (New York and London: Allen & Unwin, 1919), which contains a good discussion of the theory of descriptions. A good short discussion of logicism is contained in Arthur Pap's *An Introduction to the Philosophy of Science* (Glencoe, Ill.: Free Pr., 1962); Pap sets out the thesis very clearly, discusses its shortcomings, and suggests how it might be patched up. For a critique of psychologism, see the introduction to Roderick M. Chisholm's *Realism and the Background of Phenomenology* (Glencoe, Ill.: Free Pr., 1960).

The philosophy developed by Russell and Moore after the break with idealism can be found in Russell's *Problems of Philosophy* (London: Oxford Univ. Pr., and New York: Henry Holt, 1912) and Moore's *Some Main Problems of Philosophy* (London: Allen & Unwin, 1953). Russell criticized monism and its subject-predicate logic in many places, but perhaps the most readable criticism is in his "Logical Atomism." In that paper he discusses the philosophy of the same name, but a better introduction to the philosophy of logical atomism and the thesis of truth-functionality is J. O. Urmson's *Philosophical Analysis* (Oxford: Clarendon Pr., 1956).

The theory of descriptions was originally spelled out by Russell in his paper "On Denoting" (reprinted in his *Logic and Knowledge*, ed. by R. C. Marsh [London: Allen & Unwin, 1956]). For a recent criticism of that theory, see P. F. Strawson's "On Referring" (*Mind* 59:320–44 [1950]). Frege's position can be found in his paper "On Sense and Denotation" (trans. by Herbert Feigl in *Readings in Philosophical Analysis*, ed. by Herbert Feigl and Wilfrid Sellars [New York: Appleton, 1949]).

There are a number of good introductions to atomism and early analytic philosophy. Urmson's *Philosophical Analysis* has already been mentioned; Urmson is critical of atomism. In *The Development of Logical Empiricism* (Chicago: Univ. of Chicago Pr., 1951), Joergen Joergensen discusses Russell's atomism and Wittgenstein's *Tractatus* by way of introduction to the work of Rudolf Carnap, whom we will take up in the next chapter. But, in the case of Russell at least, there is no need to turn to commentaries. Where he is not discussing technical matters Russell is not difficult to read. His intellectual autobiography, *My Philo-*

sophical Development (London: Allen & Unwin, 1959), contains a simply written introduction to each phase of his philosophy.

There is a series of collections of essays on the work of contemporary philosophers edited by P. A. Schilpp and published by Northwestern University Press. The series contains *The Philosophy of G. E. Moore* (Evanston, Ill.: Northwestern Univ. Pr., 1942) and *The Philosophy of Bertrand Russell* (Evanston, Ill.: Northwestern Univ. Pr., 1944). These books contain essays by well-known scholars on the work of Moore and Russell; many of the essays have become classics. In addition, each book contains a reply written by the subject of the book, and a complete bibliography of the subject's work. The series also contains *The Philosophy of Alfred North Whitehead* (Evanston, Ill.: Northwestern Univ. Pr., 1941), but Whitehead's mature philosophy was developed after he left Britain to come to the United States and cannot be classified as analytic.

The Encyclopedia of Philosophy (ed. by Paul Edwards [New York: Macmillan, 1967]), contains articles on all of the philosophers and many of the problems that were discussed in this chapter; each article has a short bibliography.

There are many good textbooks of symbolic logic. An easy introduction is contained in Irving Copi's *Introduction to Logic* (New York: Macmillan, 1968). *The Development of Logic*, by William Kneale and Mary Kneale (Oxford: Oxford Univ. Pr., 1962), contains a discussion of the logical and mathematical work of Peano, Frege, Russell, and Whitehead.

CHAPTER 2

KNOWLEDGE AND MEANING

We have seen that according to the atomists the world is made up of atomic facts. Facts are actual states of affairs. Facts are independent of one another; there are no complex facts, no fact influences another fact, no fact contains another fact. True atomic propositions picture atomic facts, but true complex propositions do not picture complex facts; there are no complex facts. Complex propositions are all truth-functional compounds out of atomic propositions. There is nothing in reality corresponding to the truth-functional compounding; in reality there are only atomic facts.

But if that is the way things are, then every sentence must yield to truth-functional analysis if it is to be considered meaningful; every meaningful sentence must be equivalent to some truth-functional compound of atomic propositions. This is the challenge that faced the atomists. If atomism was to turn out to be correct, then every proposition must in some sense or other be reducible to atomic propositions and logical connectives. The proposition expressed by

John believes that the light is red,

for example, seems to picture a state of affairs that is not atomic, John's believing that the light is red. That state of affairs seems to relate John with another state of affairs, the light's being red, as the object of his belief. But, if the atomists are right, we have been misled by the grammar; if there were a state of affairs that related an individual with another state of affairs, it would be complex, and there are no complex states of affairs. Our job as analysts, consequently, will be to find the true form of the proposition expressed by the sentence "John believes that the light is red." When we have found that form we will see (the atomist supposes) that the proposition is either atomic, or a truth-function of atomic propositions.

ATOMISM AND EMPIRICISM

One sort of analysis might be this: The proposition really expressed by

John believes that the light is red

is the proposition that under certain specifiable conditions, John acts in certain ways. Dispositions to behave in certain ways is all the belief-sentence is really about. This would be an attempt at a behavioral analysis of belief sentences; we will discuss such attempts at length in chapter 4. For now it is sufficient to notice that what is being said is that the sentence displayed above expresses a proposition that would be better expressed by a sentence like this one:

> If John does not apply the brake, then John's
> heartbeat increases, and John breaks out in
> a sweat; and if there is a police car nearby
> then John applies the brake; and. . . .

This sentence describes how John might act if he believed the light to be red. Notice that the sentence is a truth-functional compound out of the atomic sentences

John applies the brake
John's heartbeat increases
John breaks out in a sweat
there is a police car nearby

and others, by means of the logical, truth-functional connectives "and," "not," and "if—then." Does the longer truth-functional sentence about John's behavior capture the meaning of the shorter belief-sentence? If it does not, if the complex proposition about what John believes cannot be completely analyzed in some such way as a truth-functional compound, then, the atomist is committed to maintaining, it does not picture a state of affairs at all, for all states of affairs are atomic, and all propositions are either atomic or truth-functional compounds. The work of the analyst (according to the atomist) is just to show how propositions can be analyzed into truth-functional compounds of atomic propositions.

There are other types of sentences besides belief-sentences that seem to require analysis. Consider sentences that seem to express propositions relating experience to things in the world around us:

Most of us, when confronted by a table, have the experience of seeing a table.

If you plunge your hand into very hot water, you will feel pain.

Such sentences seem to express propositions that picture states of affairs that relate one sort of state of affairs—experiences—with another—the existence of certain things. My experiences are related to things in the world, aren't they? I may sometimes be mistaken about what I seem to see, but usually when I have the experience of seeing a table, there is in fact a table there. We may hope that our experiences are not totally independent of the facts about existence. But if experience is related in some way to the existence of tables and chairs (the *objects* of experience), then there are complex facts in the world. It seems to be a fact, for example, that my having the experience of seeing a table is generally good evidence for the existence of a table, and if it is a fact, it seems to be a complex fact. How can the atomist handle propositions that apparently picture such complex facts?

One way would be simply to deny that sentences about the objects of experience, material objects, are atomic. We could insist that they express propositions which are truth-functional compounds of atomic propositions about experiences. The consequence would be that the relation that holds between propositions about experience and propositions about the world would be a purely logical one, and would not represent any relation between states of affairs in reality. A sentence apparently about a material object, under this view, would really be about experiences—just those experiences we would have when brought face-to-face with the supposed material object. The material object would be a sort of construct out of experiences. That makes it clear how propositions about experiences can be related to propositions about material objects; both sorts of propositions involve only experiences, and so the relation is a logical one. How do we account for the fact that my experience of seeing a table is some evidence for the existence of the table? The answer is that my experiencing the table is part of what it means for there to be a table here! Other possible experiences make up the rest of the meaning. Such an analysis of material object sentences into experience sentences is a phenomenalistic analysis in its simplest form. If such analysis succeeds, then propositions about the relation of experience to reality do not represent complex states of affairs. The experience proposition is a truth-functional part to the truth-functional whole of the material object statement. And so another possible objection to atomism would be removed.

We might, of course, have tried to do it the other way around, constructing propositions about experience out of propositions about material objects. The principle would have been the same: To show that what we had supposed to be a relation between states of affairs, or in other words a complex state of affairs, was really no more than a logical relation between propositions— that of truth-functional part to truth-functional whole. What is important to see here is that atomism requires that we make one choice or the other. Either all our atomic propositions are about experience, and propositions about material objects are truth-functional compounds out of the atomic experience propositions, or else all the atomic propositions must be about material objects, with propositions about experience to be truth-functionally constructed. There is no other way for the atomist to explain the relation that must exist between propositions about experience and propositions about material objects.

But there is still the question of which way to choose: Shall we make experience basic, and construct material objects, or shall we make material objects basic, and construct experience? That question was resolved by what can only be called Russell's empiricist bias, in favor of taking the experience propositions as atomic and basic to the construction of material object propositions. In what follows in this chapter we will discover the role empiricism came to play in analytic philosophy.

Russell seems to have been convinced that physical objects, seen traditionally as distinct from experience, were essentially unreachable, that their existence could never be known but only inferred from our experiences; that is, insofar as they are distinct from our experience, they are merely inferred entities. So much the worse for the traditional view that they are distinct from experience! They will be constructed out of experiences; that is really to say that propositions about physical objects will be shown to be truth-functional constructs out of propositions about experience. "Wherever possible replace inferred entities with logical constructions," became a slogan for the early analysts. In general, problematic entities were to be constructed out of less problematic ones, as Whitehead had constructed points out of classes of volumes of finite size. In particular, propositions about material objects were to be constructed out of propositions about experience with the help of logical connectives. But if the meaning of every sentence could be reduced to some combination of experiential statements, then empiricism must be correct, for empiricism says that all knowledge arises from experience. If the construction worked, all knowledge would be seen to be *about* nothing but experience.[1]

Russell did not hold the belief that physical-object statements were really statements about experience for long, but other analysts after him, notably Rudolf Carnap, tried to perform the construction, and their work has been of great importance if only for clarifying the issues. We must consider the work of these later writers on the subject, and so we first briefly consider Russell's work. Even before we do that, though, we should mention the work of Ernst Mach.

Mach, a German philosopher and scientist of the nineteenth century, was an empiricist. He believed that claims to knowledge must all ultimately be justified by appeal to experience. He was also a positivist; that is, he was inclined to dismiss the problems

---

1. On construction, *see* Joergen Joergensen, *The Development of Logical Empiricism* (Chicago: Univ. of Chicago Pr., 1951). Russell seems to have abandoned phenomenalism by the time he wrote *Analysis of Matter* (New York: Harcourt, 1927).

of metaphysics. Metaphysical problems—the existence of God, an afterlife, the nature of the mind—had always been taken seriously by philosophers, but, as Kant had pointed out, it is impossible to reason out the answers to such questions. Positivism is even more harsh; there are no real problems being posed here; such questions are really nonsense. The philosopher must turn his back on metaphysics, if philosophy is to make any real headway. For Mach, as for the positivists of the twentieth century, the headway that philosophy had to make was primarily in providing secure foundations for science.

Mach believed that knowledge could be, and could only be, grounded in experience. Experience he saw as the collection of atomic sensations. For every knowledge claim, therefore, it must be possible to show that that claim is really about complexes of sensations. The reconstruction proceeds through several levels: First, physical objects are constructed out of sensations, and then the self; and then on this basis other persons can be constructed. If such a construction were thoroughly satisfactory, then there would be no question whether knowledge could be grounded in experience, since whatever we have knowledge about is simply a construct out of sensations. There is, as I have pointed out above, no essential difficulty in showing the relationship of our knowledge to experience.

Gestalt psychology has made it clear to us, of course, that experience cannot be simply a collection of atomic sensations, but that presents no insurmountable problem. If Mach's project were in every other respect successful, then all that would be necessary to meet this objection would be a construction of sensations out of whatever it is that makes up experience; then everything else could be based on sensation in just the same way. The real problem for Mach seems to be the nature of the construction involved. Just what was Mach doing when he constructed a physical object out of sensations? If he was not doing metaphysics, then he was not telling us what the ultimate constituents of physical objects are. What then? It was just in regard to this question that Russell and the logical positivists, followers of Mach in the twentieth century, seemed so much better prepared than he was; it was the machinery of the new symbolic logic that made it possible to say just what was to be done in the reconstruction of knowledge.[2]

2. *See* Ernst Mach, *Analysis of Sensations* (Chicago: Open Court, 1914), chapter 1.

RUSSELL'S
CONSTRUCTION

A point in space, if you remember your mathematics, is an entity that has no dimensions. We could never discover points in experience; anything large enough to be in our field of vision would be too large to qualify as a point. How do we arrive at points, then? They must be inferences from what is in our experience. Yet there is no known way of deducing the existence of points from the data of experience. If we could substitute for these inferred entities constructions out of the data of experience, then their existence would be no problem. This new sort of point, this constructed point, which would have all the mathematical properties required of points, would be related in an obvious way to experience—it would be constructed out of it. But how was that to be done? Insofar as it was done, the achievement is Whitehead's; I quote from Russell's *Our Knowledge of the External World*:

> We have first of all to observe that there are no infinitesimal sense-data: any surface we can see, for example, must be of some finite extent. We assume that this applies, not only to sense-data, but to the whole of the stuff composing the world: whatever is not an abstraction has some finite spatio-temporal size, though we cannot discover a lower limit to the sizes that are possible. But what appears as one undivided whole is often found, under the influence of attention, to split up into parts contained within the whole. Thus one spatial datum may be contained within another, and entirely enclosed by the other. This relation of enclosure, by the help of some very natural hypotheses, will enable us to define a "point" as a set of spatial objects; roughly speaking, the set will consist of all volumes which would naturally be said to contain the point.[3]

What Russell says may be a little misleading; the object is neither to define points out of existence, nor to define them into existence. The object is, rather, to provide a way of understanding propositions which seem to be about inferred entities, points, as propositions which are in fact about certain collections of visual data. How do we know certain propositions about points to be true, when no one has ever seen a point? The an-

3. Bertrand Russell, *Our Knowledge of the External World* (London: Allen & Unwin, 1914), p. 120.

swer is, such propositions are not really about things no one has seen; they are precisely about things that have been seen. We have replaced inferred entities with constructions out of things that are known to us.

What Whitehead did for points, Russell had done for the king of France, if you remember. In place of propositions about (apparently about) the king of France, he gave us propositions involving properties (including the property of being king of France) and about everything that actually exists. The king of France is a construction, we might say, but we can say that only if we keep in mind that in each of these cases what is being constructed is a proposition, and not really the king of France in any sense. Any apparently simple proposition about the king of France is to be seen as really a logical construct out of atomic propositions about things that do exist.

Numbers also, which at one time Russell believed to have an independent existence, could be constructed; let the number one be the set of all sets containing only one thing, the number two the set of all sets containing exactly two things, and so on. Here again it is important to remember that what is really being said is that sentences about numbers can be construed as expressing sentences about sets of a certain sort. "The number of any class is defined as all the classes that are similar to it."[4]

Points, present-day kings of France, and numbers are not known to us, but they can be constructed out of what is known. It was Russell's prejudice that physical objects are also not known to us; the problem of perception became for Russell to show how propositions that purport to be about physical objects can be constructed out of propositions about what we know, namely, our sense-data.

> If physics is to be verifiable, we are faced with the following problem: Physics exhibits sense-data as functions of physical objects, but verification is only possible if physical objects can be exhibited as functions of sense-data. We have therefore to solve the equations giving sense-data in terms of physical objects, so as to make them instead give physical objects in terms of sense data.[5]

4. Bertrand Russell, *My Philosophical Development* (London: Allen & Unwin, 1959), p. 70.

5. Bertrand Russell, "The Relation of Sense-Data to Physics," reprinted in *Mysticism and Logic and Other Essays* (London: Longmans, 1918), pp. 146–47.

The prejudice betrayed is this, that while the data of the senses could be known, physical objects could not. Their existence had to be inferred from the existence of the sense-data. But, if that much is correct, it is also correct that the required inference is going to be shaky, and undermined by facts about illusions and dreams. (After all, how can we infer from our sense-data that certain physical objects exist, when the fact that we have those sense-data is consistent with the possibility of our being sound asleep?) But all of that is only true of physical objects as inferred entities. If things could be constructed out of the data of experience just as points are to be constructed out of volumes, then their existence would not be problematic, and the relationship of their existence to the facts of experience would be clear.

> . . . a thing may be defined as a certain series of appearances connected with each other by continuity and by certain causal laws. In the case of slowly changing things, this is easily seen. Consider say, a wall-paper which fades in the course of years. It is an effort not to conceive of it as one thing whose color is slightly different at one time from what it is at another. But what do we really *know* about it? We know that under suitable circumstances—i.e., when we are, as is said, "in the room"—we perceive certain colours in a certain pattern: not always precisely the same colours, but sufficiently similar to feel familiar. If we can state the laws according to which the colour varies, we can state all that is empirically verifiable; the assumption that there is a constant entity, the wallpaper, which has these various colours at various times, is a piece of gratuitous metaphysics. We may, if we like, *define* the wall-paper as the series of its aspects. These are collected together by the same motive which led us to regard the wall-paper as one thing, namely a combination of sensible continuity and causal connection. More generally a thing will be defined as a certain series of aspects, namely those that would commonly be said to be *of* the thing. To say that a certain aspect is an aspect *of* a certain thing will merely mean that it is one of those which, taken serially, *are* the thing.[6]

Thus Russell proposes an empiricist solution to the atomist's problem, how to explain the connection between the facts of experience and the facts of the physical world. He proposes to construct propositions about the physical world out of propositions about sense-data. This is a truth-functional analysis; prop-

6. Russell, *Our Knowledge of the External World*, pp. 111–12.

ositions are being analyzed into atomic propositions. One more point: Although Russell chooses as his basic entities sense-data, it would be wrong to suppose that he means by "sense-data" psychological events or mental entities. Sense-data, the data of the senses, were always, for Russell, independently existing objects. They differed from physical objects only in this respect: While it is not possible to be immediately acquainted with physical objects (Russell said), we are immediately acquainted with sense-data.[7]

CARNAP'S CONSTRUCTION

Russell had suggested how the construction might be carried out; he pointed to the construction of points and numbers as examples, and indicated the lines along which the construction of physical objects must go. He had gone further than Mach, who did not have available to him either the machinery of symbolic logic, or the examples of construction in mathematics. Russell had shown how the techniques of logical analysis might be applied to the problem. But it remained for Rudolf Carnap to make the first thoroughgoing attempt to carry out the construction.

Carnap belonged to the Vienna Circle, a loose association of scientists and philosophers, founded by Moritz Schlick in Vienna in 1923. The aim of the Circle was made known in a pamphlet circulated in 1929 and paraphrased in Joergen Joergensen's *Development of Logical Empiricism*:

> The aim is to form an Einheitswissenschaft, i.e., a unified science comprising all knowledge of reality accessible to man without dividing it into separate, unconnected disciplines such as physics and psychology, natural science and letters, philosophy and the special sciences. The way to attain this is by the use of the *logical method of analysis*, worked out by Peano, Frege, Whitehead and Russell, which serves to eliminate metaphysical problems and assertions as meaningless as well as to clarify the meaning of concepts and sentences of empirical science by showing their immediately observable content . . .[8]

7. For Russell at least, sense-data were not mental entities; they were neutral between the mental and the physical. Russell eventually abandoned the attempt to construct the physical world out of sense-data.

8. Joergensen, *The Development of Logical Empiricism*, p. 4.

The overriding concern of the Circle was to demonstrate the unity of science—that there is really only one science, physics, and that psychology can be reduced to (constructed out of) biology, and biology and chemistry to physics. The only language the scientist need speak is physical language; the only laws he requires are physical laws. The members of the Vienna Circle were known as logical positivists; they were not atomists, because atomism is a metaphysical theory, a theory about the way things are, and the positivists rejected every metaphysical theory as nonsense. The Circle had a criterion for detecting nonsense, called the verifiability criterion: If a sentence is not either tautologous (a logical truth) or self-contradictory on the one hand, or capable of being verified or falsified by experience (at least in principle), then it is nonsense. One consequence, apparently, of the criterion is that only truth-functional compounds turn out to be meaningful; another is that the basic propositions in these compounds must be empirical. It was at these points that the antimetaphysical positivists agreed with the atomism of Russell and Wittgenstein. But we will discuss this when we return to the verifiability criterion later.

Since physical language can be reduced to the language of experience, and the language of experience can be reduced to physical language—they are interreducible, Carnap claimed—it was open as to which of the two should serve as the basis of the construction of all concepts. Carnap chose in *The Logical Structure of the World* what he took to be the epistemological ordering; he chose to make experience basic, just as Mach and Russell had. But unlike Mach he did not identify such experience with sensation. Influenced by the work of the Gestalt psychologists, Carnap chose for the basic elements of his system whole slices of experience—elementary experiences—the whole of what we are experiencing at any one time. He took such experiences to be unanalyzable. It is only by grouping experiences in certain ways that we arrive at qualities, then sensations, then a visual field, then objects, and so on.

With respect to what is real and what is not, Carnap's construction claims to be neutral. The ideas of reality and unreality are themselves constructions, coming at a fairly high level of construction. Carnap calls his method solipsistic, since all concepts are to be built up out of the experience of one person. But that results simply from his choice of a basis; the construction itself makes no claims about the reality or unreality of other people, the world, etc.

In *The Logical Structure of the World*, Carnap describes his method of construction:

> In order to indicate more clearly the nature of our objective, the "constructional system," some important concepts of construction theory should first be explained. An object (or concept) is said to be *reducible* to one or more other objects if all statements about it can be transformed into statements about these other objects. . . . If *a* is reducible to *b*, and *b* to *c*, then *a* is reducible to *c*. Thus reducibility is transitive. . . .
> According to the explanation given above, if an object *a* is reducible to objects *b*, *c*, then all statements about *a* can be transformed into statements about *b* and *c*. To reduce *a* to *b*, *c* or to construct *a* out of *b*, *c* means to produce a general rule that indicates for each individual case how a statement about *a* must be transformed in order to yield a statement about *b*, *c*. . . .
> By a *constructional system* we mean a step by step ordering of objects in such a way that the objects of each level are constructed from those of lower levels. Because of the transitivity of reducibility, all objects of the constructional system are thus indirectly constructed from objects of the first level. These basic objects form the *basis* of the system. . . .
> Even though the subjective origin of all knowledge lies in the contents of experience and their connections, it is still possible, as the constructional system will show, to advance to an intersubjective, objective world, which can be conceptually comprehended and which is identical for all observers.[9]

Carnap here indicates that he will make the slices of experience the basis of his system; he needs, in addition to these elementary experiences, a relation that holds between them. Such a relation is *recollection of similarity*; a recollection of similarity holds between two elementary experiences when they are recognized as being partly similar by a comparison of a memory image of one of them with the other. On the basis of this relation other relations are defined, then quality classes of experience can be defined, and then quality classes divided into different sensory modalities (visual, tactual, etc.). The next step is the construction of temporal ordering and spatial ordering, from which physical space is constructed. Carnap outlines the rest of the construction:

9. Rudolf Carnap, *The Logical Structure of the World*, trans. by Rolf George (Berkeley: Univ. of California Pr., 1969), pp. 6–7.

To begin with, we shall discuss the method of constructing three-dimensional, *physical space*, and then we shall carry out this construction as well as the construction of the visual things which depend upon it. For the constructional system, the most important visual thing is *my body*. It will help us to give definite descriptions of the various senses, so that with its aid we can supplement the domain of the auto-psychological—the elementary experiences. Then we shall describe the construction of the *world of perception* as well as the construction of the *world of physics*, which is quite different from the former.[10]

Eventually the experiences of others are to be constructed, and finally cultural objects. There is no reason for us in this chapter to follow Carnap into the technicalities of the construction. The interested reader is referred to Carnap's book.

VERIFIABILITY

The Vienna Circle represents a resurgence of the empiricism and positivism of Mach, armed with insights provided by Russell's work in symbolic logic. Almost all the members of the Circle were scientists. Impressed by theoretical advances in physics and the foundational studies in mathematics, they had come to see the philosopher's job as the clarification of the language of science, in preparation for the unification of science. They, more than any other group of philosophers in the twentieth century, insisted on rigor and careful formulation in philosophy. What other men had suggested, they attempted to work out in detail, and often they succeeded. If positivism and the Circle's empiricism can be seen today to be untenable, that is largely because those doctrines were formulated so carefully that they could be refuted, and often the refutation of a particular doctrine came from a member of the Circle. They injected into contemporary philosophy a new sensitivity to the dialectical process. The philosopher's views would hereafter be liable to careful scrutiny and discussion. The philosopher was no longer to work at his own system like a hermit; he was to be a co-worker, a laborer working at his own special place. And the philosopher's place was the clarification of the language of science.

Philosophers had too long been working in the realm of what cannot be known. They were forever issuing bold claims about

10. Ibid., p. 191

the nature of reality, underlying existence, the identifiability of nature with goodness, the attributes of God, the duration of self, and so on. And for any claim made by anyone in any of these areas, there seemed always to be a counterclaim made by someone with just as much (or just as little) evidence on his side. It was this state of affairs that Kant had called a scandal; philosophers could not agree on anything.

It had been part of Kant's effort to show that certain of these subjects—the traditional subject matter of metaphysics—were outside the realm of philosophy, that man simply did not have the equipment to reason to an understanding in these areas. The efforts of the philosophers were misdirected; traditional metaphysics was wasting its time. But Kant never doubted that the claims of metaphysics were meaningful; the claim that there is a God is either true or false, although we are not in a position to determine which is true by philosophizing. Likewise, that the self cannot be destroyed is either true or false. The claims of metaphysics had meaning, Kant believed; it was simply that we had no rational way of determining their truth or falsity.[11]

Now the logical positivists also rejected the claims of metaphysics. But their rejection was more thoroughgoing than that of Kant; not only was metaphysics not part of knowledge, its claims were not even meaningful. Claims like "There is a God" and "The soul survives the body" described no state of affairs and were not meaningful; and, of course, since they were not meaningful, neither were their negations. Both "There is a God" and "There is no God" are meaningless; neither one is either true or false. Our knowledge originates in experience, after all; Carnap had tried to show how all our nonlogical knowledge might be reduced to statements about experience. When I make a claim to knowledge, you can always challenge it: "How do you know?" Ultimately my justification must rest on experience of some sort. It is but a short step to saying that my claim to knowledge is ultimately *about* experience, and as we have seen that is a step that was taken by Carnap.

But the claims of metaphysics cannot be justified by an appeal to experience; consequently, they are not about anything. At one stroke positivism sweeps away whole bodies of metaphysical doctrine as meaningless chatter. This move was embodied in a criterion that we have already discussed, the veri-

---

11. Kant argues his case in *Critique of Pure Reason.* Kant denied that we could *reason* to a knowledge of such things, but he did not deny their meaningfulness.

fiability criterion of meaningfulness: Only those sentences are meaningful which are in principle verifiable, or else tautologous or self-contradictory. The truth-tables of chapter 1 give us a method of determining whether a sentence is tautologous or self-contradictory. Those sentences are verifiable, of course, whose truth would make some difference to experience. Sentences whose truth or falsity could make no conceivable difference to experience are unverifiable and thus meaningless. Say, for example, what experiences would convince you that God does not exist; if no conceivable experience would convince you, then the claim that God does not exist is not verifiable, and so it is meaningless; consequently, so is the claim that God does exist. The same is true of any claim whose truth or falsity would make no difference to experience—claims about what is good, about the nature of the universe-as-a-whole, about the self. All such claims are literally meaningless; they contain no factual information, nor are they logically true or logically false. That does not mean that such sentences have no usefulness; they might be expressive of certain sorts of emotion, as poetry is. They might even be capable of inspiring men, but they do not say anything about the world. If we want to say that in virtue of their usefulness they have a sort of meaning, we must distinguish that sort of meaning from descriptive meaning. Perhaps we could talk of the expressive or emotive meaning of religious language, poetry, or ethics. The ethical theory that was the most congenial to the positivists was called the emotive theory. We will take that theory up in a later chapter.[12]

Just as the noncognitive nature of religious and ethical talk seems to follow from the verifiability criterion, behaviorism also seems to follow. Claims about the psychological states of other persons seem to be meaningful; when I say "He is unhappy this morning" what I say is surely not meaningless. But if those claims were about the subjective states of other persons, they would not be verifiable and thus not meaningful ("I can't get inside his mind"). Insofar as they are meaningful, they must be about something in experience; a good candidate is (overt, observable) behavior. Thus when I say "He believes that the light is red," what I mean is that he is behaving in certain ways, and would under certain circumstances behave in such and such

12. For a statement of the verifiability criterion, *see* Alfred J. Ayer's *Language, Truth, and Logic* (London: Gollancz, 1936), chapter 1. In the "Introduction" to the 1946 edition, Ayer reconsiders the principle.

other ways. Verifiability inclines us to behaviorism, and so lends support to the thesis that all of science can be unified under one language, for if behaviorism is true, then psychology can be put into physical language—behavior can be described in the language of physics. The claim that all knowledge can be expressed in physical language is called physicalism.[13]

Carnap did not choose the physical language for the basis of his constructional system; he chose to base the physical language on the language of experience, confident that everything higher in the construction could be reduced to physical language. Carnap accepted physicalism then, even though he believed the reduction could be carried even farther, down to the language of experience. It was not long before Carnap abandoned the belief, which had been central to his actual construction (though not to the theory), that the language of the physical world could be reduced to the language of private experience. He came to believe that if all concepts are constituted out of "my" experience, then there is no way for me to communicate with others: I would be locked into the "circle of my ideas." Since our concepts must be intersubjective, Carnap in his later work assumed that the construction of concepts, if it is to succeed, must take the physical language as basis. Since we start with something intersubjective, physical objects, there is not the problem of communication.[14] We will hear more about these developments in the chapter on epistemology.

CONCLUSION

In these two chapters we have seen the stage set for a discussion of contemporary developments in analytic philosophy. Everything that has been discussed took place between 1900 and 1930. So far the discussion has not been critical, but the chapters that follow will consist of criticism of atomistic and positivistic positions in several areas of philosophy, and a discussion of the more recent developments—positions which have grown out of or replaced those earlier positions.

13. Physicalism is defended in Carnap's "Psychology in Physical Language," in Alfred J. Ayer's *Logical Positivism* (New York: Free Pr., 1959).
14. Not all the positivists started, as Carnap did, with experience. Neurath seems to have been convinced of the difficulties involved much earlier than Carnap. Others, like Schlick, were never convinced that experience must (or could) be denied a privileged position.

In the discussion up to now we have touched on certain principles which will come in for especially close scrutiny. The fate of these principles must structure any discussion of analytic philosophy. Those principles are truth-functionality, atomism, empiricism, verifiability. All of these principles are related. *Truth-functionality* says that the truth-value of a compound sentence is dependent only on the truth-values of its component sentences, and not on something called the "meaning" of the sentence. Truth-functionality has as a corollary that only logical truths are necessarily true. This lends support to *empiricism*, in particular *logical empiricism*, whose claim is that all knowledge of nonlogical truths is reducible to experience. For if there were any necessary truths that were not merely logical (and thus trivial), then, since knowledge of such truths cannot be derived from experience (what experience tells you that something is necessarily the case?), empiricism would have to be false. Again, if truth-functionality is correct, then all compound propositions are simply truth-functional compounds of atomic propositions, and so there is no need for anything in the world but atomic states of affairs, to which the atomic propositions must correspond. Thus, *atomism* has a chance of being true. On the other hand, if *verifiability* is correct, then the statements of atomism turn out to be unverifiable, and so meaningless.

The recent history of analytic philosophy has been, at least in part, the history of these principles—principles urged originally for the clarity they seemed to bring to philosophy. Truth-functionality has simply not survived, except in certain restricted areas of scientific language. Empiricism of the phenomenalist sort we have described seems to have been shown to be untenable and to have gone out of fashion at about the same time. The useful strictures imposed by the verifiability criterion, which apparently cannot be formulated, must now depend on the intuitions of philosophers. But more of this in the proper place. In chapter 3 I will discuss the developments in epistemology, in chapter 4 those in the philosophy of mind; chapter 5 will be devoted to ethics, and chapter 6 to the philosophy of logic.

SUGGESTIONS
FOR FURTHER READING

Much of what this chapter tries to do is done better in Joergen Joergensen's *The Development of Logical Empiricism* (Chicago:

Univ. of Chicago Pr., 1951); in that book the positions of Mach, Russell, Wittgenstein, and Carnap are set out very clearly. It is such a concise book, however, that its author is obliged to treat every topic only insofar as it touches the development of logical empiricism (logical positivism and later related positions). Our concern here is much broader.

Alfred J. Ayer's *Language, Truth, and Logic* (London: Gollancz, 1936) introduced positivist thought into England; the book contains a discussion of phenomenalism and verifiability, and other topics of interest to the positivists of the time. Russell's phenomenalism is discussed in an easy way in chapter 9 of his *My Philosophical Development* (London: Allen & Unwin, 1959); he says there that he abandoned phenomenalism because of the solipsism it seemed to require.

Rudolf Carnap's construction is developed in his *Logical Structure of the World* (trans. by Rolf George [Berkeley: Univ. of California Pr., 1969]); we will talk more about the construction in the next chapter.

The adventurous reader who is curious about the fate of the verifiability criterion can look up Carl Hempel's article, "Problems and Changes in the Empiricist Criterion of Meaning." It can be found in Alfred J. Ayer (ed.), *Logical Positivism* (New York: Free Pr., 1959).

Arthur Pap's *An Introduction to the Philosophy of Science,* part 1 (Glencoe, Ill.: Free Pr., 1962), contains a good discussion of verifiability; his book *Elements of Analytic Philosophy*, chapters 7 and 8 (facsimile ed.; New York: Hafner, 1972), includes a good discussion of phenomenalism. Pap's books are always to be recommended.

PART 2

THE PROBLEMS

CHAPTER 3

THEORY
OF
KNOWLEDGE

When Russell and Moore abandoned the idealism of their teachers, they did not move directly to atomism, but to realism. Having left behind the monism of the idealists, they found it refreshing to contemplate the plurality of things in the universe. The plurality they contemplated was Platonic—it included numbers, qualities, and possibilities. In *My Philosophical Development* Russell describes the change in terms that might better be used to describe a religious conversion:

> I felt it, in fact, as a great liberation, as if I had escaped from a hot-house on to a wind-swept headland. I hated the stuffiness involved in supposing that space and time were only in my mind. I liked the starry heavens even better than the moral law, and could not bear Kant's view that the one that I liked best was only a subjective figment. . . .
> Hegelians had all kinds of arguments to prove this or that not "real." Number, space, time, matter, were all professedly convicted of being self-contradictory. Nothing was real, so we were

assured, except the Absolute, which could think only of itself since there was nothing else for it to think of and which thought eternally the sort of things that idealist philosophers thought in their books.

All the arguments used by Hegelians to condemn the sort of things dealt with by mathematics and physics depended upon the axiom of internal relations. [We have discussed Russell's attack on that axiom, in chapter 1.] Consequently, when I rejected this axiom, I began to believe everything the Hegelians disbelieved. This gave me a very full universe. I imagined the numbers sitting in a row in a Platonic heaven. (Cf. my *Nightmares of Eminent Persons*, "The Mathematician's Nightmare.") I thought that points of space and instants of time were actually existing entities. . . . I believed in a world of universals, consisting mostly of what is meant by verbs and prepositions.[1]

It was this sort of realism that Russell eventually set about to pare down through analysis. But at first he and Moore were as realistic as any recent philosopher.

REALISM

This realism was set out in Russell's *The Problems of Philosophy* and in Moore's *Some Main Problems of Philosophy*.[2] Russell moved away from many of the doctrines contained in these books, but the direction which philosophy was to take was already evident in them. In the pluralism they advocate lies the possibility of analysis. For the idealists, analysis was falsification, for analysis is taking apart, at least conceptually, and if there is really only one thing, then there is nothing to take apart. An analysis of perception, for example, involves at least two things, a perceiver and what is perceived; however these last are to be analyzed, the analysis must preserve the fact that they are two things, and not one. Thus, the analysis of perception relies on there being at least two things, related in a certain way. For the idealist the dichotomy required does not exist; there is only one thing, which cannot be understood through analysis.

1. Bertrand Russell, *My Philosophical Development* (London: Allen & Unwin, 1959), pp. 61, 62.
2. Bertrand Russell, *The Problems of Philosophy* (London: Oxford Univ. Pr., and New York: Henry Holt, 1912); G. E. Moore, *Some Main Problems of Philosophy* (London: Allen & Unwin, 1953). Although published 40 years later, Moore's book was written before, and probably contributed to, Russell's.

And so the rejection of idealism made possible philosophical analysis.

The realist analysis of perception involved at least three things for Moore and Russell: the perceiver, the perceived, and sense-data. What we are *really* aware of in perception, they wanted to say, are not the physical objects, but sense-data, which bear (we trust) certain relations to physical objects. Russell made the point in this way: When I look at a table from different angles, what I see has different and even contradictory properties. From one angle what I see is trapezoidal; from another angle what I see is rectangular; and from yet another what I see approaches being a straight line atop four legs. What I actually see changes with the angle of viewing. But surely the table itself cannot be both rectangular and trapezoidal; there must be something else that has those properties. Again if I look at the table under lights of different colors and intensities, I see different shades of color. Not all those shades of color can belong to the table: If something is brown all over, then it cannot be grey all over. So there must be something that has those shades, a different thing for each shade of color. The answer is that what we actually see are sense-data; it is the sense-datum that has the particular shape and color that we see, and the same is true for every other actually observed property of the table. There are sense-data for every sense; they intervene between us and the thing we are (indirectly) perceiving—assuming that there is something to be perceived besides the sense-data. If there are physical objects, it is by means of sense-data that we perceive them. These sense-data are probably in a causal relation to physical objects (that is, they are probably caused by physical objects), but that cannot be determined empirically, because we cannot get behind the sense-data to see to what they are related. How *do* we know, then, of the causal relation between physical objects and sense-data? Russell's answer, in *The Problems of Philosophy*, seems to be that the hypothesis of physical objects causing sense-data is the simplest explanation of the existence and order of sense-data.[3]

PHENOMENALISM

Russell was never quite happy with this inference to physical objects; he preferred, as he said, to replace inferences to un-

3. Russell, *The Problems of Philosophy*, pp. 24, 25.

known entities with constructions out of known entities.[4] And so, in his next book,[5] he suggested the construction of physical objects out of sense-data that was sketched in the last chapter. He never bothered to work the construction out thoroughly, and in later years he returned to a version of the causal hypothesis,[6] but the construction he had suggested was important to empiricism in both its atomistic and positivistic forms, as we shall see. It received its most careful formulation in the phenomenalism of Alfred J. Ayer and C. I. Lewis, and we turn our attention now to that perceptual theory.[7]

The claim that our experiences are related to physical objects which cause them is not a claim, as we have noted, that can be established empirically the way the claim that some flowers are blue can be established, nor is it a trivial or tautological claim. It is a problem, therefore, for the empiricist, for whom all meaningful, nontrivial statements can—at least in principle—be verified or refuted empirically. The answer suggested by the work of Russell and Carnap and others is to reject the causal hypothesis, and attempt to construct physical objects out of sense-data. If such a construction could be worked out, there would be a solution to the problem—no longer would it seem that we must accept the relation between sense-data and physical objects only as an unsupported inference. The problem of the external world is to be dissolved through an understanding of logical form. If we really understand sentences about physical objects, if we see through to their logical form, we will understand that they are *really* sentences about sense-data. That physical objects can be constructed out of sense-data—that propositions about physical objects are really propositions about sense-data—is the claim of phenomenalism.

Let's review what it means to say that a sentence apparently about one sort of thing is "really" about another. We saw in chapter 2 that Carnap introduced, in his *Logical Structure of the World*, a technical notion, reducibility: An object *a* could be

4. Bertrand Russell, "Logical Atomism" in *Logical Positivism*, ed. by Alfred J. Ayer (New York: Free Pr., 1959), p. 34.

5. Bertrand Russell, *Our Knowledge of the External World* (London: Allen & Unwin, 1914).

6. *See*, for example, Bertrand Russell, *The Analysis of Matter* (New York: Harcourt, 1927), chapter 20.

7. For Alfred J. Ayer's formulation, *see Foundations of Empirical Knowledge* (London: Macmillan, 1940); for C. I. Lewis's, *see An Analysis of Knowledge and Valuation* (LaSalle, Ill.: Open Court, 1947).

reduced to or constructed out of objects *b, c* if and only if a general rule could be produced that indicates how a statement about *a* could be replaced with a statement about *b, c*. Such rules are called construction rules. The apparent objects that are constructed by means of these rules are called logical constructs. Russell called the terms that seemed to refer to such constructs incomplete symbols. An example of an incomplete symbol would be one of the definite descriptions we talked about in an earlier chapter. In "The present king of France is bald" the phrase "the present king of France" does not refer to anything; it can't, since there isn't anything to which it can refer. We may be misled by this fact into all sorts of philosophical puzzles, unless we realize that it is not the sort of expression that can be expected to refer, or have meaning in isolation. It is *incomplete*; only as part of a sentence is it meaningful. And when we understand the true logical structure of the sentence we understand that it is not about the king of France, but rather about all things that do exist. It says about those things that one of them has king-of-France-hood, and is bald. It is thus both meaningful and false.

Now where a sentence contains an incomplete symbol purporting to refer to a physical object, as "There is a table in Room 303" does, it must ultimately be transformable into sentences about what is observable. We may say that sentences containing incomplete symbols which appear to refer to physical objects are transformable into sentences about, and so are "really" about, sense-data or elementary experiences. The view that this is so we have called phenomenalism. An alternative view, the view that sentences apparently about experience are really about physical objects, we may call radical physicalism. If our object is merely to show that science has only one language, then either reduction would be acceptable. If our purpose, however, is to show how knowledge of physical objects is possible, we may be inclined to try the phenomenalist reduction. For Russell, while our knowledge of physical objects is problematic, our knowledge of sense-data is direct and unproblematic; the only possible reduction, under those circumstances, is the phenomenalistic one.

How does a phenomenalistic analysis of a physical object statement proceed? Clearly enough, the phenomenalist cannot hope to convince us that an adequate analysis of a physical-object statement could consist in a conjunction of simple categorical sense-datum statements. For example,

> There is a table here ≡ I am aware of sense-datum A, and I am aware of sense-datum B, and I am aware of sense datum C, and . . .

(where "A," "B," "C," . . . refer to sense-data of various shapes, colors, and so on) is not going to work. Does the table cease to exist because my sense-data cease? If I am in Room 305, and someone asks me if there is a table in Room 306, should I reply, "No, since I am not having any of the relevant sense-data?" And how are we to decide which sense-data *are* relevant? Does the sense-datum of shape depend on my position relative to the table? And doesn't the color depend on the lighting? The point is that if there is to be an adequate phenomenalistic analysis, the sense-datum statements must be hypotheticals, and not categoricals. They must say that I feel a certain feel *if* I touch the table; I see a certain shape, *if* I am in such and such a position with respect to the table; I sense a certain color, *if* the lights are so and so. In other words, a more adequate analysis would look like this:

> There is a table here ≡ If X, then I am aware of sense-datum A, and if Y, then I am aware of sense-datum B, and . . .

There is at least one more qualification that we must observe: In this scheme, "X," "Y," . . . —the antecedents of the hypotheticals—must themselves be entirely in the language of sense-data. It would be wrong for us to suppose that we had given a sense-datum analysis, if not all the terms of the analysis were sense-datum terms. So, instead of my standing in such and such a place, and instead of the lights being so and so, the antecedents must be about it *seeming* to me that I am standing in such and such a place, and about the lights *seeming* to be so and so. Instead of talking about my touching the table, we must talk about it seeming to me that I am moving my hand in the direction of the table, and so on. In that way we restrict ourselves to talk about the way things seem to me, or about the way my experience is—that is, we restrict ourselves to the language of sense-data.

The adequate phenomenalistic analysis, then, will look something like this:

There is a table here $\equiv$ If I have sense-datum D, then
I will have sense-datum A, and
if I have sense-datum E, then
I will have sense-datum B,
and . . .

There are other important questions that may be raised about the analysis: Are the hypotheticals really truth-functional compounds? Must the list of statements on the sense-datum side of the analysis be infinite? But those questions go beyond our purpose here. The reader who would like to follow up on them is referred to the formulations of Ayer and Lewis.

The phenomenalistic construction, if it works, solves the problem of the external world to the satisfaction of the empiricist. The atomistic empiricist, who insists that all facts are independent of one another, need not be perplexed about the apparent relationship between facts about experience and facts about physical objects. If phenomenalism is right, *all* facts are facts about experience; statements about physical objects are really truth-functional constructs out of sense-datum statements. The positivist, on the other hand, does not have to explain the non-empirical, nonlogical nature of meaningful statements relating sense-data and physical objects, for if phenomenalism is right, such statements *are* logical in nature. If physical objects are constructions out of sense-data, then the verifiability criterion's requirement that all meaningful sentences be either logical or empirical will be met.

All of this worked for the wide acceptance of phenomenalism, but it was never universally accepted, and eventually it fell out of favor altogether. There are three main tenets of phenomenalism, and each of them came under serious attack: the very notion of basing one sort of knowledge on another sort (epistemological order); the idea that what we are most certain of are sense-data statements or experiential statements or statements about our own psychological states (the given); and the possibility of translating sentences about the world into sentences about experience (construction). Perhaps it is wrong to suppose that one sort of knowledge is more basic or more immediate than another, as Russell did. But even if it is not, it may be a mistake to suppose that the most immediate sort of knowledge is knowledge about our own experience. Finally, even if it were acceptable to base knowledge on experience, it might be wrong to suppose that the nature of that "basing" is construction.

THE GIVEN

Phenomenalism prefers to replace talk about physical objects with construction out of sentences about the given. The existence of such physical objects is dubitable, after all, while we can be sure of the existence of the given. If I experience a waterfall in the desert, there may be no waterfall there, but I know for sure that I am having the experience of a waterfall. Furthermore, while the properties a particular physical object will have may be doubtful, about the properties of my experience there is no doubt whatever. If, in looking at an object, I am presented with an elliptical shape, the shape of the object may not be elliptical at all, but certainly the shape in my experience is. Thus, although some of my experiences may be misleading about the world, I am not misled about the experiences themselves; they are exactly as I see them. And since my experiences are all I really ever see, I am never mistaken about what I see; any mistake lies in some faulty inference to the world of physical objects.

The possibility of mistake lies in the inference, then; about the basis of such inference—experience—there can be no mistake. Thus there is a basis of certainty supporting the structure of knowledge, a stopping point for the justification of knowledge claims. For Russell and Moore this experiential basis is in the nature of sense-data; for Carnap, in the nature of elementary experiences. In either case, it is what is called "the given."

Almost every part of this description of the given is controversial: that an experience is *something*; that an experience is something we can see, hear, etc., and moreover the only thing we can see, hear, etc.; that there is certainty in statements about such experiences. Let's confine our discussion to sense-data. Early on Russell was quite clear about sense-data being things. Sense-data were neither mental nor physical; we were directly aware only of them, and it was through their mediation that we came to know (later: construct) the world. In our knowledge of sense-data there was no possibility of being wrong. Russell maintained all three of the controversial points.

1. To take sense-data as *something* gives rise all over again to the question they were to answer: How is it that we can be in touch with the things we perceive? If sense-data are things, then what mediates our seeing of them? For if our seeing of physical objects needs to be mediated through sense-data, then it is not the facts of hallucination and dreaming that create that

need, although they point it out; normal experience calls for such mediation too. Why then does the awareness of sense-data not require such mediation? So if sense-data are things, they are of questionable value. But this is the least important objection; apparently we can deny sense-data any metaphysical status (we can deny they are things) without seriously affecting the rest of the theory of the given. We might, for example, simply take "I am aware of a red sense-datum" to mean that the speaker is experiencing red, without supposing that there must be some thing which is in experience, namely, a sense-datum which has the property redness.

2. To suppose that it is sense-data that I am aware of, or, to say it without the metaphysical implications, to suppose that what we are aware of are the ways in which we experience, contradicts what we would normally declare to be true. Normally, I would suppose that it is tables and chairs and other people that I am aware of, and not my experiences of those things. We are, of course, sometimes aware of our experiences; I am aware right now that I am seeing the numeral "12" on my watch. The problem arises from trying to make awareness of experience cover all cases, from supposing that *all* I am aware of are sense-data. Though it may be difficult to say in what way my awareness is related to a table, one thing is clear: It is an awareness of a table, and not an awareness of some other awareness. But the phenomenalist can concede even this. He does not claim that all we are aware of are sense-data; all he needs to claim is that there is some sort of distinction between things we are *immediately* aware of (sense-data, or ways of experiencing), and things we are *indirectly* aware of (physical objects, another man's thought).

3. The really important objection to the idea of the given is that it does not really provide us with a secure, absolutely indubitable basis for knowledge. This objection has come from a number of sources, among them the pragmatic tradition in American philosophy. It is found, for example, in the work of Nelson Goodman.[8] Goodman's attack is against the notion that statements about sense-data are indubitable and not subject to correction. For we might certainly be mistaken about any such statement—there is many a slip between the experience and the lip—and we might, on further evidence, even correct ourselves

---

8. Nelson Goodman, "Sense and Certainty," *Philosophical Review* 61 (1952): 160–67.

about them. We can imagine a man saying "The color I see is blue," then changing his mind and saying "The color I see is aqua." In at least one of those cases, both of which are sense-datum reports, the subject must have been mistaken, assuming that the color did not change. How then can the given be said to provide absolute certainty?

But from the fact that the statements I make may not reflect my experience, or that I might later retract my statements, it does not follow that I do not know what my experience is. If, for example, I am experiencing red and I believe that I am, then I may be said to know that I am experiencing red. It does not matter that I may be uncertain about what words to use in describing the experience; that would not cast any doubt on my knowledge of the way in which I am appeared to, but only on my knowledge of the way in which certain words are used. If this were not so, then we could never give a name to a color we had never seen before; for according to the argument if it did not already have a name for us, we could not be sure about what color we were seeing, and so, even if we gave it a name, we could not be sure to which color we had given the name, and so the name would be useless. The only sense in which we cannot know what color we are seeing when we see a previously unnamed color is in the altogether trivial sense that we cannot know a name for it.

What the objections show us, then, is that we must be careful how we construe "the given"; we must not take it in such a way that the facts of perception entail that there are intermediary objects between perceiver and perceived, and we must not take it in such a way that we are committed to the view that all we can know are our own experiences. What the objections do not show is that the given cannot serve as a stopping point for the justification of knowledge claims. They do not compel us to give up the notion of the given, but only to tidy it up. It is not about the given that phenomenalism goes wrong; phenomenalism can do just as well with the tidied-up notion of the given.

EPISTEMOLOGICAL ORDER

What requires the given, or some other basis for knowledge, is the idea of order—the idea of a structure of knowledge. How do we justify the claim that we know such and such? We justify it by appealing to something else that we know, something that will itself be justified by appeal to some other piece of knowledge. And the process of justification must come to an end, or no claim could ever be justified. We could consider this order of justification an ordering of knowledge. Phenomenalism is characterized not only by the assertion that knowledge is a structure of that sort, but, as we have seen, also by the assertion that the basis of the structure is our knowledge of the given.

The order of justification is supposed to be roughly this: Knowledge claims about institutions and social bodies are justified by reference to knowledge claims about persons (and so our knowledge of institutions and social entities is based upon our knowledge about individual persons). Claims to know facts about persons are justified by reference to claims about physical objects (their bodies, facial expressions, utterances, etc.) (and so our knowledge about persons is based on knowledge about physical objects). And claims to know about physical objects are justified by reference to claims about sense-data, experience, the given. All of knowledge is thus a structure resting on the data we gather through our senses.

This very neat picture began to lose favor during the forties. The prevailing lack of patience with it found expression in the arguments advanced by J. L. Austin at Oxford in the late 1940s and early 1950s. They were primarily directed against the views of Alfred J. Ayer, who was at the time the leading spokesman in Britain for logical positivism and phenomenalism. Austin's arguments seem to revolve around this point: We do not normally *have* to justify statements about physical objects or other persons; such statements are not normally in doubt. We are as sure as we are of anything that, under good conditions, it is a chair we see. No one would ordinarily call such a claim doubtful, or require justification of it. And the appeal to the possibility of deception, which is meant to show that such statements are doubtful, is in complete disregard for the way in which the word "deception" is actually used. There are ways of distinguishing perceptions that are liable to be deceptive from those that are not. For example, we may be deceived about what appears to be a ship in the distance, but we are not likely to be deceived about what is before us in good light when we are sober and well. We do not ordinarily justify knowledge claims, and we do not ordinarily need to.[9]

9. J. L. Austin, *Sense and Sensibilia*, ed. by G. Warnock (Oxford: Clarendon Pr., 1962), pp. 115–19.

No one who has been exposed to Austin's arguments will remain insensitive to the fact that careful consideration of the ways in which we use words is crucial to philosophical argument. But it is by no means clear that Austin "did in" the idea of epistemological order. As Ayer has pointed out,[10] it is largely a tribute to Austin's persuasiveness that it is quite widely believed that his arguments refuted the possibility of an order of justification. In point of fact they do not accomplish their mission. Even if we set aside cases of hallucination and illusion there remains the question: What relation does my knowledge of my own experiences bear to my knowledge concerning those things of which they are experiences? What relation does my knowledge that I am having a table-like experience bear to my knowledge that there is a table here? This is a question we can ask without calling the existence of anything whatever into doubt, that is, we can justify our claims to knowledge—our claim to know that the table is here, for example—without supposing that they are doubtful. This does not seem to be the point at which phenomenalism goes wrong; even if we are seldom called upon to justify our knowledge claims, the fact remains that we can justify many of them, and that there seems to be an order in which such justification proceeds.

CONSTRUCTION

There remains only the assumption that physical objects are constructs out of sense-data. To be a construct in this sense is not, if you will remember, the same as being built out of, or having as spatial parts, sense-data, though some writers have seemed close to saying that. What is involved is rather this: To say that a is a construct out of b and c is to say, as we have seen, that the whole meaning of statements about a can be given without any mention of a in statements about b and c. Statements which seem to be about a are seen then, after analysis, to be about b and c. In such cases a-statements would be true if (and only if) a certain group of b- and c-statements were true. And since it is not merely a matter of fact that these statements are related in this way, but a matter of meaning, we may say that the b- and c-statements give an analysis of the meaning of

10. Alfred J. Ayer, "Has Austin Refuted the Sense-Datum Theory?" in his *Metaphysics and Common Sense* (San Francisco: Freeman, Cooper, 1969), p. 148.

the *a*-statement. Suppose that A is the *a*-statement involved, and B, B′, and B″ are the *b*- and *c*-statements involved. Then the statement

A if and only if (B and B′ and B″)

will be *analytically true*, or true just in virtue of the meanings of the words used in the statement, if the *b*- and *c*-statements do in fact analyze the meaning of the *a*-statement. And if for every statement about *a* there is such a statement which says that it is true if and only if certain statements about *b* and *c* are true, and that statement is analytically true, then we can say that *a* is constructed out of *b* and *c*. It is important that these statements that link *a* with *b* and *c* be analytically true; otherwise, it would not be right to say that the *b*- and *c*-statements give the whole of the meaning of the *a*-statements. This is crucial to the phenomenalist claim: The whole meaning of physical-object statements is given by collections of, or conjunctions of, sense-datum statements. Consequently, it must be solely in virtue of the meanings of the words involved that the physical-object statement is equivalent to the sense-datum statements. And so, if the phenomenalist is right, there is, for every statement about a physical object, an analytically true statement to the effect that the physical-object statement is true if and only if certain sense-datum statements are true. It is in this sense that physical objects are constructs out of sense-data.

There are two main points about this account which are controversial: One is very specific, namely, whether any such statements relating physical-object statements and sense-datum statements are ever analytically true; and one is very general, whether analyticity itself is not simply a confused notion. We will take the more general controversy first.

1. Analytically true statements are supposed, by the people who believe that there are such things, not to add anything to our knowledge about the world; whatever might be the case in the world, such statements remain true. Logical truths, or tautologies, for example

A if and only if A

are analytic; and where *a* is any individual that exists,

a is *a*

is also analytic. The result of substituting in a logical truth one of two definitionally equivalent terms for the other is also analytically true, however, so that the notion of analyticity is much broader than the notion of logical truth. Suppose, for example, we define "2" as meaning the same as "1 plus 1":

$$2 = \text{def. 1 plus 1.}$$

We know that

1 plus 1 is 1 plus 1

is analytically true, since it is a logical truth, of the same form as "*a* is *a*". But then

2 is 1 plus 1

is also analytically true, resulting from the substitution in a logical truth of one term ("2") for another ("1 plus 1") with which it is definitionally equivalent. Similarly,

1 plus 1 plus 1 is 1 plus 1 plus 1

is a logical truth; and so

2 plus 1 is 1 plus 1 plus 1

is analytically true, resulting from the logical truth by a substitution like the one we performed above. Furthermore, if we define "3" like this:

$$3 = \text{def. 1 plus 1 plus 1}$$

it is not hard to see that

2 plus 1 is 3

also turns out to be analytically true. If we were to continue in this way, we would soon come to the conclusion all of the truths about the addition of integers are analytic truths; that is equivalent to saying, as we said in the first chapter, that they are all reducible, by means of definitions, to logical truths. Notice that according to our definition of construction, we could say that all of the positive integers can be constructed out of 1 and the operation of addition. Although it might sometimes be tedious, we could say anything we wanted to say about any integer in statements about sums of 1, without mentioning that integer.

Analytic truths, then, include all logical truths, and all truths that result from logical truths by the substitution of definitionally equivalent terms. Statements that are true, but not true by definition or logic, we can call synthetic truths. *Synthetic* truths are supposed to convey information about the world; the fact that they are true cannot be learned just by contemplating the terms involved. Corresponding to these two types of truth are analytic and synthetic falsehoods. An analytic falsehood is either a logical falsehood—a contradiction—or the result of substitution of definitions in a logical falsehood. Synthetic falsehoods include all other falsehoods. Both of the following are simple synthetic statements:

Friction causes warmth.

Lincoln was the fourth president of the United States.

The first happens to be true, and the second false.

Now the thesis of truth-functionality says among other things that all necessary truths are instances of logical truth, along with the substitution of definitionally equivalent terms. It says that all necessary truths are analytic; none of them tells us anything about the world. The thesis of phenomenalism—that statements relating physical objects to sense-data are analytic—is just one aspect of this more general claim. The claim that all necessary truths are analytic is important to empiricism for this reason: If necessary truths could be synthetic, they could be informative about the world, but since necessary truths cannot be grounded in experience—what experience or experiences would justify the conclusion that such and such is necessarily so?—there would be some information we could acquire about the world which would not be grounded in experience. But empiricism is first and foremost the claim that all of the knowledge we have about the world is grounded in experience, and so it must reject the possibility that necessary truths can be synthetic. The alternative is that all necessary truths are analytic, and consequently convey no information about the world; they are trivial in that sense. That is the alternative for which contemporary empiricism has opted. Since phenomenalism proposes to show how statements relating physical objects to sense-data, statements which by their very nature cannot be grounded in experience, are analytically true, phenomenalism is an important alternative in the theory of knowledge, for empiricists. But I want only to call your attention to the fact that the notion of analyticity underlies much of the thought of empiricists and phenomenalists.

This notion has come under fire from pragmatically-oriented philosophers like Quine, Goodman, and Morton White.[11] The

11. W. V. O. Quine, "Two Dogmas of Empiricism" and Morton White, "The Analytic and the Synthetic: An Untenable Dualism" are both reprinted in *Analyticity*, ed. by James Harris and Richard Severens (Chicago: Quadrangle, 1970); Nelson Goodman, "On Likeness of Meaning," *Analysis* 10 (1949): 1–7.

point is that no statement is absolutely secure; it is similar to the point argued earlier against the certainty of statements about the given. No statements are necessarily true, and so no statements are analytic. Every statement is liable to revision in the face of the facts, and consequently, every statement says something about the world. There are some statements that are less likely to be revised than others, but no statement is absolutely immune to revision. One of the key arguments is that the very notion of analyticity is confused and cannot be spelled out; at least it cannot be spelled out without using some word, like "synonymy" or "definitional equivalence," the understanding of which presupposes an understanding of analyticity.[12]

But the reply to this seems simply to be that all definitions must stop somewhere; not every word can be defined. If we try to define every word, then we are going to end up in circularity. If analyticity can be defined in terms of definitional equivalence, but definitional equivalence cannot be defined without making use of the notion of analyticity, what we should conclude is not that both notions are confused, but rather that one of them must remain undefined. The idea of analytically true statements continues to unsettle a great many philosophers, but there does not seem to be an acceptable argument to show that the idea is a confused or dangerous one.[13]

Phenomenalism will fail, of course, if analyticity fails, but we have not seen any reason why analyticity must fail. We turn, then, to the more specific objection to the idea of construction of physical objects out of sense-data.

2. This objection, denying the possibility of finding the particular analytically true statements necessary for phenomenalism was raised by Roderick Chisholm.[14] Chisholm's argument was directed in particular against the attempt by C. I. Lewis to carry out the translation of physical-object statements into sense-datum statements in his book, *Analysis of Knowledge and Valuation.* The attempt fails because of certain facts about "perceptual relativity." In Chisholm's words:

---

12. *See* in particular Quine's "Two Dogmas," pp. 32–43.
13. The best-known reply to Quine is P. F. Strawson and H. P. Grice's "In Defense of a Dogma," reprinted in the Harris and Severens collection.
14. Roderick M. Chisholm, "The Problem of Empiricism," reprinted in Robert Swartz, ed., *Perceiving, Sensing, and Knowing* (Garden City, N.Y.: Doubleday, 1965), pp. 347–54.

The roots of the difficulty are the familiar facts sometimes referred to as "the relativity of sense-perception." Whether a material thing will ever present, say, a red appearance or sense-datum depends partly upon the thing and partly upon the conditions under which it is observed. If one knew that the thing were red and that the lighting conditions were normal, one could predict that, to a normal observer, the thing would present a red appearance. . . . To calculate the appearances with complete success, it is necessary to know both the thing-perceived and the (subjective and objective) observation conditions, for it is the thing-perceived and the observation conditions working jointly which determine what is to appear. Professor Lewis believes that "This thing is red" entails as analytic consequences an unlimited number of statements referring solely to what might appear. But the facts of "perceptual relativity" suggest that it doesn't entail *any* statement about sense-data; they suggest that a sense-datum statement is entailed only when "This thing is red" is taken in conjunction with another thing [physical-object] statement referring to observation conditions. The translatability thesis requires that both the observation-conditions and things-perceived be definable in terms of what might appear. But the facts of perceptual relativity indicate that it is the joint operation of things-perceived and observation conditions which determines what is to appear; hence the task of an empiricist would seem to be similar to that of an economist who hoped to define both supply and demand in terms of possible prices.[15]

The problem is this: If a sentence P about physical objects can be translated into sentences about sense-data, S, S′ S″, . . . or to put it another way, if the statement

P if and only if S and S′ and S″ . . .

is analytically true, then the sentence P entails all of the sense-datum sentences S, S′, S″, etc. If P is true, then each of the sense-datum sentences must be true. If the translation of "This thing is red" includes, among other sense-datum sentences, "I am having a red sense-datum," then the latter statement is entailed by the former; if the first is true, then the second cannot be false. All of this is required of the phenomenalist construction. But the fact is that the first does *not* ensure the second; in fact, any physical object statement is consistent with the falsity of any sense-datum statement whatever. To see this we need

15. Ibid., pp. 348–49.

only realize that we might not, for example, be facing in the right direction, or we might have our eyes closed, or our visual apparatus might have become defective.

Moreover, any attempt to patch up the analysis by making sense-datum statements conditionals which read "If I am in such and such a condition, *then* I have a red sense-datum" has this defect: The "if" part of the sentence, the antecedent, must either be in terms that include talk about the conditions of physical objects—the lighting, my visual apparatus—or else solely in terms of sense-data. If we take the first option, we have not given a sense-datum analysis of physical-object statements, for the language of the supposed sense-datum statements is only partly the language of sense-data; it is also partly the language of physical objects. So we have not, on that option, succeeded in constructing physical objects out of sense-data.

If, on the other hand, we take the second option, we end up with an analysis entirely in the language of sense-data. In that case, as we saw, the truth of the physical-object statement is compatible with the falsity of the sense-datum statements that are supposed to analyze it. And so in this case too the construction fails; and if you have the patience to follow the reasoning in the following short passage from Chisholm's paper, you may come to see more clearly why it fails. To understand the passage, it is necessary to be clear on this point: If the statement P entails the statement R, then no matter what other statement S we conjoin with P, P & S will also entail R. In other words, if

If P then R

is analytically true, then so is

If P & S, then R.

Consequently, if the conjunction of P and S does not entail R, then P does not entail R. Now we are ready for Chisholm:

> One of Lewis's examples is the thing statement:
>   (P) There really is a doorknob in front of me and to the left.
> One of the complicated sense-datum statements which are analytic consequences of this might be:
>   (R) If I should seem to see such a doorknob, and if I should seem to myself to be initiating a certain grasping motion, then in all probability the feeling of contacting a doorknob would follow.

All these statements about what seems to me to be so, and about what I feel, should be understood as being in the language of sense-data.

> According to Professor Lewis, R is an analytic consequence of P; or, in other words, P entails R. But again, if P entails R, then it is logically impossible that there be a statement S, consistent with P and such that P and S entail not-R. Hence, if there is such a statement S, P does not entail R. Is there, then, such a statement S?
>
> It should be remarked that we are not asking whether there is such a statement S which is true. For Professor Lewis's theory concerns the *meaning* of thing statements, what is certifiable *a priori* by reference to logic and the meaning of terms. If there is a statement S, which in conjunction with P entails not-R, then, whether or not S is true, the theory is mistaken.
>
> Clearly there are many such statements S. One might be:
>
> > (S) I am unable to move my limbs and my hands but am subject to delusions such that I think I'm moving them; I often seem to myself to be initiating a certain grasping motion, but, when I do, I never have the feeling of contacting anything.
>
> This statement in conjunction with P entails not-R. There is no reason to suppose that S is inconsistent with P. Hence it is false that P entails R. . . .
>
> Thus it remains to be seen in what sense any sense-datum statement can be regarded as an analytic consequence of "This thing is red" or "That is a doorknob."[16]

If Chisholm is right in all this, it seems reasonable to suppose that the construction of physical objects out of sense-data, required by phenomenalism, will have to be set aside.

In light of these facts, we retreat from phenomenalism. We discovered that most objections were not conclusive; we were not obliged to dismiss the notion either of the given or of epistemological order. One objection does seem to be conclusive, however—the objection by Chisholm that we have just been discussing. No phenomenalist has ever successfully met the objection; Lewis himself seemed to concede the point in his reply.[17] That objection requires that we dismiss the possibility of constructing physical objects out of sense-data. We must retreat from

16. Ibid., p. 351.
17. C. I. Lewis, "Professor Chisholm and Empiricism," also in the Swartz volume, pp. 355–63.

phenomenalism, apparently, but we need not retreat from the ideas of epistemological order and the given.

RECENT DEVELOPMENTS

A theory of knowledge that retains the presupposition of epistemological order and a form of the given is the one developed by Chisholm himself. For Chisholm the principles that relate facts about ways of appearing (what we have been calling facts about sense-data) and our psychological states, including facts about what we take to be the case (Chisholm calls these facts directly evident), with facts about physical objects and other persons (what Chisholm calls the *indirectly* evident) are not analytic. Since they are not, and since they hold necessarily, they must be statements of a sort whose possibility is denied by empiricists—synthetic necessary statements. The principles of evidence that Chisholm lists tell us that states of affairs of various sorts bear such and such various degrees of evidence, and that certain cohesive groups of states of affairs each having at least a certain degree of evidence confer additional evidence on one another. In this way certain states of affairs attain the degree of evidence necessary to be called states of affairs *known* to obtain. I may not say that I know that there is a table here, for example, unless there is a certain amount of evidence for there being a table here; and there would not be that evidence unless *there being a table here* were supported by facts about the ways in which I am appeared to, and belonged to a group of states of affairs which tended to support one another.

While evidence is necessary for knowledge, there are other things that are necessary too. What is known to an individual S must be evident to him, but it must also be believed by him, and it must be true. This provides a three-part definition of "S knows that p"; according to Chisholm, S knows that p provided that (1) S believes that p; (2) it is true that p; and (3) it is evident for S that p.[18] This definition is not so unusual; a number of philosophers have offered similar three-part definitions of knowledge as true justified (or evident) belief. But a recent paper by Edmund Gettier has shown all such definitions to be incorrect. Gettier constructs a counterexample to the defini-

18. Roderick M. Chisholm, *Theory of Knowledge* (Englewood Cliffs, N.J.: Prentice-Hall, 1966), p. 23.

tions; that is, he describes an (imaginary) situation in which the three parts of the definition hold for some S and some proposition *p*, and then shows that in that situation we would not say that S knows that *p*. The situation he described was something like this one: Suppose a neighbor asks to borrow a certain book, and I agree to lend it to him; I tell him to pick it up from my desk that afternoon. After locating the book, I put my favorite bookmark in it as a reminder, and leave it on my desk. A few weeks later I want to recover it and go accordingly to my neighbor's office where I find my book lying upon his desk, with my bookmark in it, in just the tattered condition in which I lent it to him. I leave a note for him, take the book, and leave.

The question is: Did I *know* that it was my book lying on his desk? Certainly I believed that the book on his desk was mine, and certainly I had good evidence for that belief: the condition of the book; the bookmark; the fact that I had lent it to him. Let us suppose in addition that the book was indeed mine. Does it follow that I *knew* the book to be mine? Gettier would say that I do not. Let us assume that the following was the course of events between the time I left the book and the time I recovered it: Someone happened upon the book before my friend arrived, and stole it; my friend arrived, saw that there was no book on my desk, and went elsewhere to borrow it; the condition of the book he borrowed rather closely resembled the condition of my book; he placed into that book the bookmark he found on my desk, which had fallen out of my book when the thief took it; the thief happened by my neighbor's desk, and, imagining the book he saw there to be in better condition than mine (which it was not) traded the two books, and left the bookmark in the book he left with my neighbor. If you have followed all that, you understand that it is my book that ends up on my neighbor's desk with the bookmark in it. But it is wrong, Gettier would argue, to say that I *know* that it is my book, for the reasons I have for believing that it is my book— perfectly good reasons, by the way—are some of them based on false beliefs; for example, that my neighbor took the book from my desk. The fact of the matter is that my book ended up on his desk almost by chance. I cannot be said to *know* that it is my book, since I would have thought the other book was mine if I had found it there. And by all rights I *should* have found it there. But although it would seem to be wrong to say that I know that the book is my book, the three parts of the definition are fulfilled: I believe that it's my book, it is my book, and it is evident that its my book. If the definition had been correct, then from the fact that the three clauses were fulfilled it would follow that I knew that the book was mine. But I didn't know it; my belief in that case was not knowledge, since the evidence for it rested on certain beliefs which were false even though they were evident (even though my neighbor did not borrow the book, I had good evidence for his borrowing it, since he asked to borrow it, it disappeared from my desk, and later it was on his desk). So the definition is not correct. Other, more sophisticated definitions have also been shown to be inadequate; so far there is no general agreement about a definition. Since the definition connected Chisholm's principles of evidence with knowledge, we may say that in the absence of an adequate definition, Chisholm has not given us a complete theory of knowledge.[19]

SUGGESTIONS
FOR FURTHER READING

There are a number of reasonably good introductions to the analytic theory of knowledge; for a brief introduction there is Arthur Pap's *Elements of Analytic Philosophy* (facsimile ed.; New York: Hafner, 1972) and Roderick M. Chisholm's *Theory of Knowledge* (Englewood Cliffs, N.J.: Prentice-Hall, 1966).

There are also a number of good anthologies. *Meaning and Knowledge*, edited by Richard B. Brandt and Ernst Nagel (New York: Harcourt, 1965) is perhaps the most comprehensive, covering the entire field. Robert Swartz's *Perceiving, Sensing, and Knowing* (Garden City, N.Y.: Doubleday, 1965) is devoted to the problem of perception; some of the classic articles in the sense-datum controversy can be found there, as well as a full statement by Lewis of his phenomenalism. *Perception and the External World*, edited by R. J. Hirst (New York: Macmillan, 1965) covers the same ground a little differently, and includes selections from older philosophers and from well-known psychologists.

A selection of works by analytic philosophers that would complement this chapter include: Bertrand Russell's *Problems of*

19. The Edmund Gettier paper, "Is Justified True Belief Knowledge?" can be found in *Knowing*, ed. by Michael Roth and Leon Galis (New York: Random, 1970), along with commentaries and replies by various authors. In that collection there is a reformulation by Chisholm of his definition.

Philosophy (London: Oxford Univ. Pr., and New York: Henry Holt, 1912) and his *Our Knowledge of the External World* (London: Allen & Unwin, 1914); G. E. Moore's *Some Main Problems of Philosophy* (London: Allen & Unwin, 1953); Alfred J. Ayer's *Foundations of Empirical Knowledge* (London: Macmillan, 1940); C. I. Lewis's *Analysis of Knowledge and Valuation* (LaSalle, Ill.: Open Court, 1947); J. L. Austin's *Sense and Sensibilia*, edited by G. Warnock (Oxford: Clarendon Pr., 1962); Roderick M. Chisholm's *Perceiving: A Philosophical Study* (Ithaca, N.Y.: Cornell Univ. Pr., 1957) and W. V. O. Quine's "Two Dogmas of Empiricism" (reprinted in his *From a Logical Point of View* [Cambridge: Harvard Univ. Pr., 1953]).

Concerning sense-data, we can turn to the indicated books of Russell and Moore, as well as Moore's "Visual Sense Data," reprinted in the Swartz volume, and the work of C. D. Broad—see, for example, "The Theory of Sensa," taken from his *Scientific Thought* (London: Routledge, 1923) and also reprinted in the Swartz volume. In the P. A. Schilpp volumes, *The Philosophy of G. E. Moore* (Evanston, Ill.: Northwestern Univ. Pr., 1942), *The Philosophy of Bertrand Russell* (Evanston, Ill.: Northwestern Univ. Pr., 1944), and *The Philosophy of C. D. Broad* (New York: Tudor, 1959), there are criticisms of the theories of perception of these three men, and replies from each of them.

C. I. Lewis's exposition of phenomenalism is generally considered to be the most thoroughgoing; it appears in his *Analysis of Knowledge and Valuation*. The Chisholm criticism and the Lewis reply mentioned in this chapter both appear in the Swartz volume.

The best-known attack on the analytic-synthetic distinction is Quine's "Two Dogmas of Empiricism"; the relevant part can be found in the Brandt and Nagel anthology as "A Dogma of Empiricism." That volume also contains a reply by P. F. Strawson and H. P. Grice, "In Defense of a Dogma." Several articles relating to the Gettier-problems of the definition of knowledge are contained in the Michael Roth and Leon Galis anthology *Knowing* (New York: Random, 1970).

To the interested reader with some time to spend I would recommend: Russell's *Problems of Philosophy*; the Brandt and Nagel volume (especially Ayer on phenomenalism and Quine on the analytic and the synthetic); the Swartz volume (but notice that the general level of difficulty is much higher for the articles in that volume); Chisholm's *Theory of Knowledge*; and *The Encyclopedia of Philosophy* (ed. by Paul Edwards [New York:

Macmillan, 1967]) articles "Perception," "Phenomenalism," "Realism," and "Sensa," all by R. J. Hirst, and "Analytic and Synthetic Statements" and "Empiricism," by D. W. Hamlyn.

In addition there are some good general anthologies of philosophy which contain many of the relevant articles; I have in mind especially Joseph Margolis (ed.), *An Introduction to Philosophical Inquiry* (New York: Knopf, 1968), and Paul Edwards and Arthur Pap (eds.), *A Modern Introduction to Philosophy* (New York: Free Pr., 1973), but there are many others.

CHAPTER 4

PHILOSOPHY
OF
MIND

. . . So that after having reflected well and carefully examined all things, we must come to the definite conclusion that this proposition: I am, I exist, is necessarily true each time that I pronounce it, or that I mentally conceive it.[1]

But some care is needed in using Descartes' argument. "I think, therefore I am" says rather more than is strictly certain. It might seem as though we were quite sure of being the same person today as we were yesterday, and this is no doubt true in some sense. But the real Self is as hard to arrive at as the real table, and does not seem to have that absolute, convincing certainty that belongs to particular experiences. When I look at my table and see a certain brown colour, what is quite certain at once is not "I am seeing a brown colour," but rather, "a brown colour is being seen." This of course involves something (or somebody) which (or who) sees the brown colour; but it does not of itself involve that more or less permanent person whom we call "I." So far as immediate certainty goes, it might be that

1. René Descartes, *Meditations*, Meditation 2.

the something which sees the brown colour is quite momentary, and not the same as the something which has some different experience the next moment.[2]

THE MENTAL AND THE PHYSICAL

In *The Problems of Philosophy*, Russell had supposed that the perceiver—the "something which sees"—is something we can be aware of in experience. That "something" he called the subject of experience. An act of awareness had both a subject and an object; the object was, typically, a sense-datum through which we could have knowledge of material objects. All this could be learned by contemplating an act of awareness—my seeing the table, for example. In contemplating that act I become aware of the subject (that which sees the table) and the object (perhaps a brown sense-datum of such and such a shape).

What cannot be learned by reflecting upon such an act, according to Russell, is that the subject of that act is the same as the subject of some other act. That is, we cannot learn through contemplating such acts that the subject of my seeing the table is the same as the subject of seeing the coatrack. We are aware of the subject in experience, but the subject we are aware of might be different in each experience.

Russell came eventually to abandon this position. He came to think that the problem of relating mind and matter would turn out to be unsolvable if we began with irreducible subjects or perceivers and irreducible physical objects. He had suggested that physical objects might be constructed out of sense-data; it struck him that the same technique might be applied to the mental entity which he had been calling the subject. The sense-data out of which both the mental and the physical were to be constructed were themselves neither mental nor physical, but rather neutral. William James had held a similar theory, and had called it neutral monism. Organized in one way, the sense-data are supposed to constitute material objects; subjects, or minds, are just the same sense-data organized in another way. Here is the project in Russell's words:

2. Bertrand Russell, *The Problems of Philosophy* (London: Oxford Univ. Pr., and New York: Henry Holt, 1912), p. 19.

So long as the "subject" was retained there was a "mental" entity to which there was nothing analogous in the material world, but, if sensations are occurrences which are not essentially relational [relating a perceiver and an object] there is not the same need to regard mental and physical occurrences as fundamentally different. It becomes possible to regard both a mind and a piece of matter as logical constructions formed out of materials not differing vitally and sometimes actually identical. It became possible to think that what the physiologist regards as matter in the brain is actually composed of thoughts and feelings, and that the difference between mind and matter is merely one of arrangement. I illustrated this [in the *Analysis of Mind*] by the analogy of the Post Office Directory, which classifies people two ways, alphabetical and geographical. In the first arrangement a man's neighbors are those who come near him in the alphabet; in the other they are those who live next door. In like manner, a sensation may be grouped with a number of other occurrences by a memory-chain, in which case it becomes part of a mind; or it may be grouped with its causal antecedents, in which case it appears as part of the physical world. This view affords an immense simplification and enables us to regard the traditional problem of the relation of mind and matter as definitively solved.[3]

Russell's solution, then, to the "problem of the relation of mind to matter" was that the relation involved is that of two logical constructs with the same constituents. Since the subject, or the mind, is constructed out of sense-data, Russell is here denying what he had earlier maintained—that the subject is "given" in experience. Carnap, too, in *The Logical Structure of the World*, denied that we are aware of a subject, or that the subject is given in experience. According to Carnap, "the given is subjectless."[4] For Carnap the basic elements of the construction—both the construction of "the self or my mind" and the construction of "the mind of the other"—are his elementary experiences. Apparently we begin our discussion of the problems of mind from roughly the same point we began, in the last chapter, our discussion of the problem of knowledge of the world.

3. Bertrand Russell, *My Philosophical Development* (London: Allen & Unwin, 1959), p. 139.
4. Rudolf Carnap, *The Logical Structure of the World*, trans. by Rolf George (Berkeley: Univ. of California Pr., 1969), p. 64.

BEHAVIORISM

The outstanding problem, from Carnap's point of view, was the choice of the basis, as we have seen in another chapter. If the basis is autopsychological, that is, if the world I live in is a construct out of my own elementary experiences, as it was supposed to be in the *Logical Structure*, then it becomes impossible to communicate with others. My sentences are about my experiences, and since no one else can have my experiences, my sentences are in principle unverifiable by anyone else. Given the construction on an autopsychological or solipsistic base, it follows that no two men are ever talking about the same thing.[5] This led us, after a careful investigation in the last chapter, to conclude that what was wrong was the idea of construction itself, and not the choice of a basis. Carnap, however, assumed that the difficulty was in the choice of elementary experiences as basis, and maintained the hope of carrying out the construction with some other basis.

But even if we substitute some other basis the problem remains of constructing the subject out of that other basis. The world of physical objects suggests itself as a basis; it is intersubjectively accessible, and besides, the language of physics was supposed to be the unifying language of science. When Carnap turned from the solipsistic, autopsychological, phenomenalistic basis, he turned to the physical basis which was being urged by his co-worker Neurath. The problem of the subject became, in a construction on a physical basis, the problem of constructing subjects out of physical objects, that is, the problem of reducing talk about subjects to the physical language. A successful reduction of this kind we can call philosophical behaviorism. According to Carnap:

> . . . we intend to explain and to establish the thesis that every sentence of psychology may be formulated in physical language . . . [that is, that] all sentences of psychology describe physical occurrences, namely, the physical behavior of humans and other animals. This is a sub-thesis of the general thesis of physicalism to the effect that physical language is a universal language, that is, a language into which every sentence may be translated.[6]

5. Carnap makes this point in the "Introduction" to the second edition of the *Logical Structure*.
6. Rudolf Carnap, "Psychology in Physical Language," in Alfred J. Ayer, ed., *Logical Positivism* (New York: Free Pr., 1959), p. 165.

Physicalism claims that physical language is "universal and intersubjective"; the problem for the physicalist in establishing behaviorism is to show just *how* sentences about myself and my psychological states and sentences about other persons as well might be reduced to sentences about physical objects. We may illustrate how it is to be done with an example taken from Carnap:

> Example: I assert the sentence P1:
> "Mr. A is now excited."

Our problem now is: *what does sentence P1 mean?* Such a question can only be answered by the presentation of a sentence (or of several sentences) which has (or which conjointly have) the same content as P1. The viewpoint which will here be defended is that P1 has the same content as a sentence P2 which asserts the existence of a physical structure characterized by the disposition to react in a specific manner to specific physical stimuli. In our example, P2 asserts the existence of that physical structure of Mr. A's body (especially of his central nervous system) that is characterized by a high pulse and rate of breathing, which on the application of certain stimuli, may even be made higher, by vehement and factually unsatisfactory answers to questions, by the occurrence of agitated movements on the application of certain stimuli, etc.

If, now, the content of P1 goes beyond that of P2, the component not shared by the two sentences is not testable, and is therefore meaningless. If one rejects the interpretation of P1 in terms of P2, P1 becomes a metaphysical pseudo-sentence.[7]

Carnap compares the sentence P1 with the sentence "This wooden support is firm." P1 is psychological; the sentence about the wooden support is not. Both, according to Carnap, entail sentences about observable physical properties. The sentence about the wooden support entails sentences about the size, shape, and feel of the support under specified circumstances; P1 entails sentences about Mr. A's behavior under specified circumstances. The whole content, in fact, of these two sentences can, if Carnap is right, be given in physical language: The wooden support withstands heavy loads without undergoing any noticeable distortions of size or shape; as for Mr. A, our entire meaning is that his body is characterized by a high rate of breathing and a high pulse, and some other things of that sort.

7. Ibid., pp. 170–74.

This, of course, is merely an outline of how the reduction would go; if the philosophical behaviorist is right, it can be carried out in all the necessary detail. B. F. Skinner, the prominent American behaviorist, makes the claim in his book *Beyond Freedom and Dignity* that that book "could have been written for a technical reader without expressions of [a psychological] sort.... Acceptable translations are not out of reach." That, of course, is the claim of philosophical behaviorism: All talk about minds, or selves, or thoughts, or desires—all so-called psychological talk— can be translated into the physical language.

INTENTIONALITY

Construction of the subject on an experiential base had this defect in common with all construction on an experiential base: It seemed to preclude the possibility of communication. Construction of the subject on a physical base did not seem to have that problem; it suffered instead from a different problem—the problem of intentionality.

Here are some examples of psychological sentences:

> I am thinking about a walnut desk.
> Henry believes that Martin will come.
> Hugo is afraid of dictators.

It is sentences of these sorts that behaviorism claims to be able to translate into the physical language. These sentences have a characteristic, however, which sentences in purely physical language do not seem to have; each of them is about something besides the subject of the sentence—a walnut desk, Martin, dictators, and, more importantly, those other things need not exist for the sentence to be true! I may certainly think about walnut desks, even though there aren't any; Henry may believe that Martin will come, even though Martin passed away last evening; and if Hugo has his way, there won't be any dictators—but he may nevertheless remain afraid of dictators. We will call this property of sentences—being about things which need not exist for the sentence to be true—intentionality; it is a property that physical sentences do not have.

The notion of intentionality was explored by Franz Brentano, best known as the teacher of Husserl. Brentano was searching for a criterion that would enable him to circumscribe the subject matter of psychology. He did not, however, treat intentionality as a property of sentences. He considered it, rather, a property of the relation the subject of such sentences bore to the (possibly nonexistent) object of his thought, belief, fear, desire.

> The common feature of everything psychological, often referred to, unfortunately, by the misleading term "consciousness," consists in a relation that we bear to an object. The relation has been called intentional; it is a relation to something which may not be actual but which is presented as an object. There is no hearing unless something is heard, no believing unless something is believed; there is no hoping unless something is hoped for, no striving unless something is striven for; one cannot be pleased unless there is something that one is pleased about; and so on, for all the other psychological phenomena.[8]

If intentionality is indeed a characteristic of the relation between a subject and the object of his psychological state, and if it is a characteristic that no relation between physical object has, then any attempt to reduce the psychological to the purely physical must necessarily leave something out—the intentional aspect. And if it leaves out an aspect that is apparently so important, behaviorism must surely be false; it is *not* possible to translate all sentences of psychology into sentences of physical science.

Let's see how this objection to behaviorism could be rephrased as a discussion of sentences. Intentionality, let us say as we said at the beginning, is a property of sentences; some of the things mentioned in such sentences need not exist for the sentence to be true. No sentence of physics is intentional in this sense; for any sentence expressing a relationship between two physical objects to be true, each of those objects must exist.

I am thinking about Pegasus

may be true, even though there is no Pegasus; but the sentence

I am to the left of Pegasus

cannot be true, since there is no Pegasus for me to be to the left of. *Being to the left of* is a relation that holds among physical objects; so no sentence that says of two things that one is to the left of the other can be true unless both things exist. No

---

8. Franz Brentano, *The Origin of Our Knowledge of Right and Wrong,* trans. by R. Chisholm and E. Schneewind (New York: Humanities Pr., 1969), p. 14.

such sentence is intentional, therefore, nor is any other sentence that expresses a relationship among physical objects. Consequently, it stands as an objection to behaviorism, which is a claim about the possibility of translating sentences of psychology into sentences in physical language, that any such proposed translation must leave out the intentional feature of psychological sentences.

Carnap's solution to the problem of intentionality finds its roots in Wittgenstein's *Tractatus*: Belief-sentences, and all other psychological sentences, are really sentences about sentences. Instead of saying that S believes that *p*, we might simply give the behavioral equivalent of a sentence which says that S is in a belief relation to "*p*"—that is, to the sentence that says that *p*. All this is darkly hinted at in the *Tractatus*; Carnap spelled it out in this way:

John believes that *p*

goes over, roughly, into

There is a sentence "*q*," which translates "*p*," and John is disposed to give an affirmative response to the question "*q*?"

In other words, for some sentence which is equivalent to "*p*", John exhibits belief-behavior toward that sentence. For example, to determine whether someone believed that it is raining, we might translate the sentence "It is raining" into his language, perhaps as "Es regnet," and then ask him "Es regnet?" To say then that he does believe that it is raining is just to say that he would reply affirmatively to such a question. But if such an analysis of belief is correct, then belief-sentences can be rendered in physical language, since all that is involved in the analysis are descriptions of behavior that would take place under specified conditions. The important point concerning the intentionality of belief-sentences is that instead of having to talk about nonexistent objects, like Pegasus, we can restrict ourselves to talk about existent words, like "Pegasus." Such words, and the sentences in which they occur, are to be seen as collections of physical objects—marks on paper, or sounds. If the analysis is correct, then there never were any "facts of intentionality" with which to deal; belief-sentences, insofar as they are meaningful, are not about nonexistent things, but rather about sentences and words. To say

John believes that Pegasus is a winged horse

is just to say

There is a sentence "q," which translates
"Pegasus is a winged horse," and John is
disposed to give an affirmative response
to the question "q?"

And to say that is not to talk about Pegasus, but rather to talk about a sentence with the word "Pegasus" in it.

Furthermore, it is not difficult to see how this solution might be extended to other psychological sentences. First we can translate

The sentence "p" says for S that q

("The sentence 'Es regnet' says for Hans that it is raining") along these lines:

If S believes that q, and only if he does,
then he will respond in the affirmative
to "p?"

This translation depends on the previously given translation of belief. And now we can suggest how any psychological sentence is to be translated; fear, desire, hope, and the others can all be translated as in the following translation of a fear-sentence:

John is afraid that p

says simply that

For some sentence "q", John has a fear-
relation to "q" and "q" says for him that p.

Being in a fear relation to a sentence, we may suppose, means to exhibit certain sorts of behavior in the face of that sentence.

We have here then a behavioral account of psychological sentences that meets the objection that psychological sentences are intentional, and so cannot be translated into the language of physical behavior. It does that by showing that psychological sentences are to be understood in a way that is not intentional: They are not about objects that possibly don't exist; they are about words and sentences, and behavior toward those words and sentences.

The intentionalist position, formulated as an objection to this whole behavioral analysis of meaning and mind, can be found in the work of Roderick M. Chisholm.[9] Carnap has not succeeded, Chisholm argues, in analyzing out the intentional element in psychological or meaning sentences; his analysis fails because it is impossible to give a set of physical conditions which occur when and only when a certain belief occurs. If that is so, then since sentences about meaning cannot be analyzed without talking about belief (or some other psychological state), no set of physical conditions can be found which will occur when and only when the meaning sentence is true. Thus every physicalistic analysis of belief-sentences, meaning sentences, and consequently any psychological sentences must fail, and so the behaviorist analysis of mind and meaning fails.

Chisholm argues in this way: There are whole sets of circumstances under which we would be likely to answer affirmatively to a question "*p?*" when we did not believe that "*p*" was true. We might do that, for example, if we thought it would help a friend. On the other hand I would, under some circumstances, not be likely to respond in the affirmative, even though I did believe that *p*. That might be the case if I thought that answering in the affirmative would bring harm to someone I loved. Furthermore, the question "*p?*" might not even be in a language that I understood. That required us to add the qualification that the question be in my language, and that it be a translation of the English question "*p?*" in my language. But to talk about *my* language is just to talk about the language that I understand, and understand-sentences are intentional, just as belief-sentences are—we cannot eliminate the intentional by introducing a new intentional term. We come eventually to see that there are great, possibly insurmountable, difficulties in the way of a behavioristic analysis of belief and other psychological sentences.

This difficulty touches many points of the positivist program: If behaviorism fails, then physicalism fails; if physicalism fails, then the unity of science fails, and truth-functionality and extensionality remain to be established. A similar crisis revolved around the failure of phenomenalism, and it became necessary to switch to a physicalistic basis; it is not clear how the corresponding failure of physicalism could be skirted.

It is important to notice that Chisholm's argument does not depend on his saying very clearly just what the intentional prop-

9. Chisholm discusses intentionality in a number of papers; there is a section of his book *Perceiving: A Philosophical Study* (Ithaca, N.Y.: Cornell Univ. Pr., 1957) devoted to the problem.

erty of sentences is. That, as it turns out, has been very difficult to do, and Chisholm has been forced to reformulate his definition a number of times. It is still not generally agreed that he has succeeded in saying what intentionality is. I said above that a sentence is intentional if some of the things mentioned in the sentence need not exist for the sentence to be true, but that was only meant to suggest what intentionality is; it is certainly not a definition. If it were, then the sentence

> Pegasus does not exist

would be intentional, since Pegasus—mentioned in that sentence —need not exist for the sentence to be true; in fact it can only be true if he does not exist! But that sentence is certainly not intentional in the desired sense, and it is clearly not psychological. So it is not sufficient for intentionality that the sentence could be true without entailing the existence of something mentioned in the sentence. Chisholm began, therefore, with a somewhat more adequate formulation:

> A simple categorical statement (for example,
> "Parsifal sought the Holy Grail") is intentional if
> it uses a substantival expression (in this instance,
> "the Holy Grail") without implying either that there
> is *or that there isn't* anything to which the expres
> sion truly applies.

By requiring that intentional sentences also not entail the *nonexistence* of something mentioned in the sentence we rule out our sentence about Pegasus as nonintentional.

> And we could say that a compound statement . . . is
> intentional if any of its components would be inten
> tional when asserted categorically.[10]

But this formulation is also not adequate. It is not a sufficient condition of a sentence being psychological that the sentence contains a substantival expression and does not entail either the existence or the nonexistence of anything to which the expression applies, for many statements of possibility also would turn out to be intentional on that formulation.

> It's possible that there is a performance
> this evening

10. Roderick M. Chisholm, "Intentionality and the Theory of Signs," *Philosophical Studies* 3 (1952): 57.

does not imply either that there is a performance, or that there isn't one. If intentionality is to be a mark of the psychological, therefore, we still haven't said what intentionality is. The reader who is interested in pursuing this question is referred to the bibliography at the end of this chapter.

But even though the question of the proper formulation of the notion of intentionality is still open, Chisholm's objection to the behaviorist reduction of psychological sentences is pretty widely accepted. Quine, for example, who would prefer to be on the behaviorist side in this, acknowledges what he calls Brentano's thesis—that psychological sentences cannot be translated into physical sentences. But his conclusion differs from Chisholm's. Since these sentences cannot be translated into the language of physical science, they are not essential to a description of the world as it really is:

> if we are limning the true and ultimate structure of
> reality, the . . . scheme for us is the austere
> scheme that knows no quotation but direct quotation
> and no propositional attitudes but only the physical
> constitution and behavior of organisms.[11]

Belief, hope, and fear, and other psychological states are all propositional attitudes. What Quine seems to be saying here is that whatever other usefulness psychological sentences might have, they are not among the sentences we must use if we are to describe the world.

Clearly then it is not an immediate consequence of the irreducibility of psychological sentences that we must give up behaviorism; we might find a way of giving up the psychological sentences instead. But that alternative seems arbitrary, unless we can find some sense of "really goes on" in which psychological sentences do not describe what really goes on.

PERSONS

If sentences about our mental states are not translatable into sentences about the way our bodies move, then we might conclude that behaviorism is false. And if behaviorism is false, then the physicalistic claim that psychology is part of physics is false,

11. W. V. O. Quine, *Word and Object* (Cambridge, Mass.: Wiley & M.I.T. Pr., 1960), p. 221.

for either there will be no science of the mental, or else the principles of that science will not be derivable from the laws of physics—they will not even be *translatable* into the language of physics.

If physicalism is false, what follows from that? One thing we might conclude is that there are at least two sorts of things in the world: Those which can be the subjects of psychological sentences, and those which can be the subjects of physical sentences (sentences in the language of physical science). In

John is thinking about his family

we might suppose that the subject term "John" refers to a mental entity, a mind that is doing the thinking; and that in

John is covered with a rash

the subject term "John" refers to a physical body.

On this view a human being would not be one thing, but two, a mind *and* a body. Things that go on "in" the mind are related to things that go on in the body. Very often, for example, I find my body buying a soda just after my mind develops a craving for one, and then, after my body has finished the soda, my mind is happy.

Seeing the human being as two parts—mind and body—requires us to give some explanation of the connection between the two. Does my mind influence my body? If so, how? If not, then why are they related at all? Such problems can seem to be insoluble, and it was one of behaviorism's advantages that it avoided such problems, since if behaviorism is true, if all mental talk can be reduced to physical talk, there really is no reason to suppose that a human being is both mind and body, or anything other than a body.

But even though the case for behaviorism has been undermined, it is still not necessary to conclude that a human being has two parts, mental and physical. P. F. Strawson, for example, in his paper "Persons,"[12] has claimed that persons are a basic sort of entity—and not any kind of construct—and an entity of a peculiar sort: A person can be the subject of either sort of sentence, psychological or physical.

Some of the things in the world have this property: The only true sentences of which they can be the subject (that is, the only

12. In *Minnesota Studies in the Philosophy of Science*, vol. 2, ed. by Herbert Feigl, Michael Scriven, and Grover Maxwell (Minneapolis: Univ. of Minnesota Pr., 1958), pp. 330–53.

true sentences having as subject terms words referring to those things) are sentences in the physical language. Such things, rocks and tables, for example, are bodies—physical bodies. But some things can be the subjects of either physical *or* psychological true sentences; those things are persons. A rock can be over two feet high and moving south at seventy miles per hour; it cannot be aware of those facts. I mean that a rock cannot be what "that individual" refers to in the sentence.

That individual is aware of moving south,

if that sentence is to be true, nor can any other physical object. A person can also be over two feet high and moving south at seventy miles per hour; the person can, moreover, be thinking about those facts.

A person is one thing, according to Strawson, namely, a person. And persons and physical objects are different sorts of things: To persons both psychological and physical predicates apply; to physical objects only physical predicates apply. Here there is no problem of relating the mental and physical parts of a human being; they are not distinct things, at all. What is the relationship between the physical and the psychological, on this view? Strawson does say that it is on the basis of their (physical) behavior that we ascribe psychological predicates to other persons. We cannot, after all, get "inside their thoughts"; their thoughts are not ours. When we say of someone that he is thinking of home, or is depressed, or is amused, it is on his behavior—including his overt linguistic behavior—that we base our claims; that is what lent behaviorism whatever force it had. But we do not apply psychological predicates to ourselves in the same way. It is not on the basis of my behavior that I decide that I am depressed, or amused, or thinking about home—though we can sometimes learn interesting things about our mental state by observing our own behavior. The point is that we do not usually need to reason from our behavior to justify claims about our own mental states. In Strawson's theory of persons this fact plays an important role: What characterizes psychological predicates, and distinguishes them from physical predicates, is precisely this, that they can be ascribed to others on the basis of some evidence (the behavior) and to oneself on the basis of no evidence whatever. That we are in a certain mental state is something that we can usually know directly without evidence. But physical predicates which can be ascribed to persons must be ascribed to all persons, myself and others, on exactly the same sort of evidence. I learn that someone else is tall in just the same way that I learn that I am tall; "is tall" is therefore a physical predicate. Strawson seems to have provided us with another mark for distinguishing the mental from the physical.

THE IDENTITY THEORY

We have, so far, been assuming that behaviorism is false, but many philosophers today accept behaviorism as a partial explanation of the facts of our mental life. Even though there are certain sorts of psychological sentences that cannot be given a behavioral translation, there are certain sorts that can—psychological sentences about mental states that take place over longer periods of time, and tend to be dispositions. Being depressed, for example, is not exactly something that happens, or something that I do; to be depressed is to be in a state that might well be simply equated with dispositions to behave in certain ways under certain circumstances. Being in love is another such state, and so is being happy, being angry, disliking, and so on. Sentences about such states, the claim is, can be given a purely behavioral translation. But what about other psychological sentences—sentences about thinking, believing, fearing, supposing, and so on? We said earlier that if behaviorism couldn't handle such sentences, then physicalism fails. There is a way, however, to bring a sort of physicalism back in; we can call that sort of physicalism materialism. The way is this: Apply behaviorism where it is applicable (to mental dispositions, for example); in the case of mental events of the other sorts, for which behaviorism is not applicable, take those events to be strictly identical with certain physical events going on in the brain. Such a theory is called materialistic because it seems to allow us to suppose that there are in the world only physical objects, just as pure behaviorism would have; it allows us to suppose that there are neither minds which go together with physical objects to make up human beings, nor persons which are different from physical objects. On this view, also known as the identity theory, human beings are just physical objects; psychological sentences about human beings are either about their behavior, or about events taking place in their brains. The theory has a certain amount of popular adherence; you will find it set out as a scientifically established truth in certain books on physiology.[13]

It would be too much to suppose that whenever we talk about mental events, we *mean* neural, physical events, and the identity theory does not claim that we do. After all, we talked about thoughts and beliefs and hopes long before anyone even knew what a neural event is like. So the theory is not claiming that certain psychological predicates mean the same thing; rather, the claim is that mental events just are physical events. A man might not know that the thirty-seventh president of the United States was the author of the famous Checkers speech of 1956; and so he could not mean the same thing by the two expressions "the thirty-seventh president" and "the author of the Checkers speech." Nevertheless, the thirty-seventh president and the author of the speech are one and the same. Similarly even though mental expressions ("thinking about home") and physical expressions ("undergoing neural event N") do not mean the same, that by itself does not show that the identity theorist is wrong, for his claim is simply that both expressions refer to the same thing.[14]

Sentences about mental events, then, are about certain physical events; those mental events are just physical events of a certain sort. Nevertheless, because of the difference in meaning, we cannot *translate* a sentence about a mental event into the corresponding sentence about a physical event without a loss of meaning. Still, insofar as sentences about mental events are about anything in the world, they are about the physical events in the brain; and anything over and above that contained in the mentalistic sentence is really about nothing at all.

And so, if the identity theory is right, psychology is not just about behavior; it is about neural events as well. The theory cannot be verified empirically, of course; can you tell by looking that this thought you are having is the same as some event in your brain? But it could be empirically refuted. It depends on the supposition that each type of mental event is accompanied by a certain sort of neural activity. If it could be shown that at least sometimes mental events occur without the corresponding neural activity, then the identity theory would be refuted; for

13. For example, in D. E. Wooldridge's *The Machinery of the Brain* (New York: McGraw-Hill, 1963). chapter 12.

14. A good discussion of the identity theory is Jerome Shaffer's "Could Mental States be Brain Processes?" *Journal of Philosophy* 58 (1961): 813–22.

mental events to be identical with neural events it is at the very least necessary for the neural event to occur each time the appropriate sort of mental event occurs.

If it is not refuted in this way, it is difficult to see how it might be refuted. As a philosophical claim it bears a certain resemblance to the claim that God *is* the universe (even though men mean different things by "God" and "the universe"); it is not easy to tell just what would count as evidence for either claim. Perhaps the identity theory is especially difficult to grapple with because its philosophical implications are so few. For example, it is a materialistic theory, and yet it is compatible with the view that there are other things in the universe besides physical objects—for mental events might be just events going on in the physical brains of men, and yet men might be essentially different from physical objects, in the way that Strawson supposes that they are. On the other hand, even if the identity theory is false, materialism need not be; it might be that mental events are essentially different from physical events, and yet that both sorts of event involve only physical objects. The job of establishing a materialist position must be distinct, therefore, from the job of establishing the identity theory. But if all this is true, then it might be to the point to question the importance of that theory.

SUGGESTIONS
FOR FURTHER READING

Some particularly clear introductions to the problems of mind and body are: Jerome Shaffer's *Philosophy of Mind* in the Prentice-Hall Foundations of Philosophy series (Englewood Cliffs, N.J.: Prentice-Hall, 1968; in the same series part of Richard Taylor's *Metaphysics* [Englewood Cliffs, N.J.: Prentice-Hall, 1963; a new edition is forthcoming] is devoted to the philosophy of mind); chapter 12 of Arthur Pap's *Elements of Analytic Philosophy* (facsimile ed. [New York: Hafner, 1972]) and chapter 20 of his *Introduction to the Philosophy of Science* (New York: Free Pr., 1962); A. R. White's *Philosophy of Mind* (New York: Random, 1967); and, for the more serious student, C. D. Broad's *Mind and Its Place in Nature* (London: Routledge, 1925) and C. J. Ducasse's *Nature, Mind, and Death* (LaSalle, Ill.: Open Court, 1951). These last two are older books, but they contain invaluable discussions of the various positions.

I do not know of any truly comprehensive anthology of work by analytic philosophers in the philosophy of mind. A. G. N. Flew (ed.), *Body, Mind, and Death* (New York: Macmillan, 1964) is a historical collection, but it does contain essays by Ayer, Ryle, U. T. Place, and others. Short collections of papers by contemporary philosophers are V. C. Chappell (ed.), *Philosophy of Mind* (Englewood Cliffs, N.J.: Prentice-Hall, 1962), Donald F. Gustafson (ed.), *Essays in Philosophical Psychology* (Garden City, N.Y.: Doubleday, 1964), and Stuart Hampshire (ed.), *Philosphy of Mind* (New York: Harper, 1966). Papers discussing the relationship of minds and machines can be found in Sidney Hook (ed.), *Dimensions of Mind* (New York: Colliers, 1961) (along with essays on many of the positions that have been discussed in this chapter) and Alan Ross Anderson (ed.), *Minds and Machines* (Englewood Cliffs, N.J.: Prentice-Hall, 1964). Hook's anthology contains papers on the identity theory, as do C. V. Borst (ed.), *The Mind-Brain Identity Theory* (London: Macmillan, 1970) and John O'Connor (ed.), *Modern Materialism* (New York: Harcourt, 1969). There is an extensive bibliography in Herbert Feigl's *"Mental" and the "Physical"* (Minneapolis: Univ. of Minnesota Pr., 1967), which contains Feigl's long and important "The 'Mental' and the 'Physical'," as well as a postscript.

The attempt to "construct" minds took several forms. Neutral monism was set out by William James in his *Radical Empiricism* (New York: Longmans, 1912), and it seems to have been adopted by Bertrand Russell in *Our Knowledge of the External World* (London: Allen & Unwin, 1914), and in *Analysis of Mind* (New York: Macmillan, 1921). The sensations out of which Mach would construct the mind (and everything else) in *Analysis of Sensations* (New York: Dover, 1959) and perhaps also Carnap's elementary experiences may qualify as neutral, being "neither mind nor matter"; if that is so, it is in spite of the fact that Carnap calls his elementary experiences "psychological objects." The *behaviorist* construction, wherein all statements about mental events would find analysis as statements about behavior, is related to the slightly older behaviorism of J. B. Watson in *Behaviorism* (New York: Norton, 1930), in which mentalistic statements about feelings and emotions and so on are not analyzed but simply dismissed. (That position, I suppose, must be considered a philosophical position, but it is important for the reader to distinguish philosophical behaviorism from the methodological behaviorism which would simply limit the psychologist's area of investigation to behavior.) Something like behaviorism is developed in Gilbert Ryle's *Concept of Mind* (New York: Barnes & Noble, 1949); Ryle's book has the distinction of being both influential and readable, and I recommend it to the reader. P. F. Strawson's position is set out in his book *Individuals* (London: Methuen, 1959); it is not an attempt at construction.

There have been a number of important articles. Hempel's "The Logical Analysis of Psychology" in which Hempel argues for physicalism and C. I. Lewis's "Some Logical Considerations Concerning the Mental" are both in Herbert Feigl and Wilfrid S. Sellars (eds.), *Readings in Philosophical Analysis* (New York: Appleton, 1949). Carnap's "Psychology in Physical Language," discussed in this chapter, appears in Alfred J. Ayer (ed.), *Logical Positivism* (New York: Free Pr., 1959). P. F. Strawson's "Persons" appears in a number of places, including his own *Individuals*. The important papers on the identity theory are collected in the anthologies on that topic mentioned above. Jerome Shaffer's "Recent Work on the Mind-Body Problem" (*American Philosophical Quarterly*, 1965) is an excellent discussion, and makes as good a starting place in the reading as any. Chisholm has several papers on intentionality; the more recent ones tend to be inaccessible unless you have read the earlier ones. "A Note on Carnap's Meaning Analysis" (*Philosophical Studies* 6 [1955]: 87–89) comments directly on an attempt by Carnap to give a behavioral analysis to the notion of meaning; Carnap replies in a note reprinted as an appendix to his *Meaning and Necessity* (2d ed.; Chicago: Univ. of Chicago Pr., 1956).

For a systematic attack on the problem, the reader might start with Bertrand Russell's *Problems of Philosophy*, and then read his *Analysis of Mind*, Ryle's *Concept of Mind*, Strawson's *Individuals*, and Shaffer's "Recent Work on the Mind-Body Problem." There are a number of good articles in *The Encyclopedia of Philosophy* (ed. by Paul Edwards [New York: Macmillan, 1967]), especially Shaffer's "Mind-Body Problem."

CHAPTER 5

ETHICS

In trying to determine whether a particular action is the right one, we may consider the act in isolation, independently of the consequences of the act, or we may pay attention to the consequences of the act. Philosophies of right action may be distinguished along these lines: Some argue that the rightness or wrongness of an action is to be determined according to characteristics the action itself possesses, and that the consequences of the action do not affect the basic moral character of the action; and some argue that *only* the consequences of an action are relevant for determining whether the action is right or wrong. Among the latter philosophies must be included *utilitarianism*, which received its classical formulation in the nineteenth century in the work of John Stuart Mill, and before him in the work of Jeremy Bentham. Mill describes this ethical philosophy in his *Utilitarianism*:

> The creed which accepts as the foundation of morals "utility" or the "greatest happiness principle" holds that actions are right

in proportion as they tend to promote happiness; wrong as they tend to produce the reverse of happiness. By happiness is intended pleasure and the absence of pain; by unhappiness, pain and the privation of pleasure.[1]

Strictly speaking, utilitarianism is less than that; it is the doctrine that an action is right if it produces the most *good* (for the most people). Many utilitarians have thought that the most good was the most happiness, as Mill did, but others have suggested different candidates for the highest good—beauty, for example. Mill's utilitarianism, in which happiness is assumed to be the highest good, would more correctly be called "hedonistic utilitarianism." There are two important questions facing this sort of utilitarianism, and most ethical discussions since the turn of the century have revolved about these two questions. The one that has generated by far the more controversy, controversy largely independent of its relevance to utilitarianism, is the question of the status of "Happiness is the highest good" and similar statements. Are they factual statements, subject to some sort of verification? Are they logical truths? Are they analytic or true by definition, or are they perhaps neither true nor false, but merely expressions of feeling? The second question has been how to reformulate the principle of utilitarianism so that it is adequate to what we know to be obviously right and obviously wrong. Much of contemporary ethical discussion can be understood best by reference to these two problems; consequently, this chapter will be devoted to tracing the course of those problems in twentieth-century analytic philosophy. To begin with the first problem—what is the status of "happiness is good?"— we must return to the philosophers against whom Russell and Moore rebelled just before the turn of the century—the idealists.

PRINCIPIA ETHICA

For at least some of the British idealists of the late nineteenth century the job of ethics was well defined; it was to show how ethics is rooted in the nature of the universe, how what-should-be is grounded in what-is. Their investigations are of no other interest to us than this: They supposed that value could some-

---

1. John Stuart Mill, *Utilitarianism* (Indianapolis: Bobbs-Merrill, 1957), p. 10.

how be reduced to fact, that "it *ought* to be the case that *p*" goes over somehow into "it *is* the case that *q* and *r* and *s*."

Here is a rather simple-minded example, which I introduce only to clarify the notion of a reduction of values to facts. Let's agree that if God has a plan for the universe, then that he does is among the facts that there are. Now the reduction I have in mind proposes that

> it ought to be the case that *p*

means

> *p* has good consequences;

and that

> *x* is good

means

> The existence of *x* is in God's plan.

The complete translation, then, of "it ought to be the case that *p*" (a value statement) would be

> The consequences of *p* are in God's plan,

and that is a statement of fact. It was in some such way as this that values were supposed, by the idealists, to be reducible to facts.

Now, utilitarianism does not presuppose either that values can or that they cannot be reduced; some utilitarians have supposed that such a reduction is possible, others have thought not. In rough outline, a utilitarian version of the reduction of values to facts might go like this: The statement

> One ought to do *p*

just means

> *p* has better consequences than any alternative action

and that

> the consequences of *p* are better than the consequences of *q*

means

> the consequences of *p* contain more happiness than do the consequences of *q*.

The complete translation, then, of "One ought to do *p*" would be

> The consequences of doing *p* contain more
> happiness than do the consequences of any
> alternative action.

In this way the utilitarian who believed that it was possible might try to show that the meaning of "good" and "better" could be given solely in terms of factual considerations about the presence or absence of happiness. Every hedonistic utilitarian believes that happiness is good; what this reductionist approach adds is the claim that happiness is part of the *meaning* of "good."

G. E. Moore, in his *Principia Ethica*,[2] tried to show that such a reduction could never succeed. Ethical properties are not natural properties, in the sense in which the idealists thought they were; the motto of Moore's book is a quotation from Bishop Butler: "Everything is what it is, and not another thing." To identify an ethical property with a nonethical property, he reasoned, is a mistake. He labelled this mistake the naturalistic fallacy, and he attempted to demonstrate that it *is* a mistake or fallacy by means of an argument known as the open question argument: Suppose someone were to suggest that goodness was to be identified with some natural, or nonethical property, say, happiness. If he were right, then it would not be open, to anyone who understood both terms, to ask "Is happiness good?" just as it would not be open to anyone who understood the terms "bachelor" and "unmarried" to ask "Are bachelors unmarried?" But of course it is open (so Moore would argue), even to someone who understood both terms, to ask "Is happiness good?" We can expect a man who perfectly understands both terms to be greatly enlightened upon finding out either that happiness is, or that happiness isn't good. Thus happiness and goodness are not the same property. In the terms of our discussion of the identity theory in the last chapter, it may be that "good" and "happy" apply to exactly the same states of affairs; nevertheless, those terms cannot have the same meaning.

Since for any nonethical property X the question "Is X good?" remains open, Moore concluded that goodness is not identical with *any* nonethical properties. And since the way the world is can be described in nonethical—or natural—terms, no ethical

---

2. G. E. Moore, *Principia Ethica* (Cambridge: Cambridge Univ. Pr., 1903).

statement can be derived from statements about the way the world is. There is an essential gap between fact and value.

Another way of underlining that gap is to claim for the notion of goodness unanalyzability; all other ethical terms are to be analyzed in terms of goodness, but goodness itself is not to be analyzed in terms of anything.

> If I am asked "What is good?" my answer is that good is good and that is the end of the matter. Or if I am asked "How is good to be defined?" my answer is that it cannot be defined, and that is all I have to say about it.[3]

If goodness cannot be analyzed, then in particular it cannot be analyzed in terms of natural (factual, descriptive, nonethical) properties. And since all other ethical terms can only be analyzed in terms of goodness, no ethical notion is analyzable into entirely nonethical notions. Ethics constitutes a realm to itself, if Moore is right, and is not a part of science or of any other discipline.

I have been using "nonethical" and "natural" interchangeably. Moore seemed to have in mind that there is a world of natural properties—color, size, weight and so on—and natural relations —is taller than, is desired by, is in front of. His point was that we cannot give the meaning of "goodness" in terms of such properties and relations. Part of the problem, of course, is to say just what a natural property is without begging the question. We cannot define a natural property as one in terms of which it is impossible to define goodness, because that would make Moore's thesis true but trivial. The point is to define *natural property* without making reference to goodness. If that could be done, then Moore's thesis would be a significant one.

Moore himself never quite succeeded in saying what natural properties are. No doubt he had in mind something like what we have in another place called physical properties, or something like what others have called observational properties, but it is not certain that anyone has ever made clear how physical or observational properties are different from properties of other kinds. In any case, Moore's thesis comes down to this: Goodness is a nonnatural property. Since happiness *is* a natural property, according to Moore, goodness cannot be identified with happiness. Thus the claim that happiness is good is a sub-

3. Ibid., p. 6.

stantial claim; whether it is true or false, it is certainly not true by definition.

Moore was himself a utilitarian; he identified the rightness of an action with the goodness of its consequences, although he didn't identify goodness with anything else at all, as we have seen. He accused Mill of the naturalistic fallacy because he believed that Mill had tried to define goodness in terms of happiness. Many have felt that the accusation was misdirected, and that Mill did not argue that "goodness" meant happiness. Whether or not Mill was guilty of committing the naturalistic fallacy, there were some who did commit it; Moore's most important contribution to ethical thought may have been to point out that fallacy, and in doing so to focus attention on the problem of the meaning of ethical terms.

EMOTIVISM

If goodness is not an empirically observable property, how do we come to know whether a particular state of affairs is good or not? If it is not a property that we can apprehend visually, like color or shape, not a property that we apprehend by hearing, touching, smelling, tasting, then how *do* we become aware that anything has the property? If we are inclined to believe that all knowledge arises in experience and is based on observable properties, we may be led to declare that we cannot have ethical knowledge. Thus an empiricist who accepted Moore's thesis might deny the possibility of ethical knowledge. But if we are inclined to believe, as a *logical* empiricist does, that all *meaning* is based on the meanings of observation terms, things will go even worse for ethics. For now the consequences of accepting Moore's thesis will be a denial of the *meaningfulness* of ethical claims; and in fact the logical positivists, who hold that only those statements which are either logical or empirically verifiable are meaningful, came to think of ethical language as being literally meaningless.

The reasoning is simple enough: Goodness is not analyzable in terms of any empirically observable properties (Moore's thesis); only those nontrivial sentences are meaningful whose meaning can be given in sentences about empirically observable properties; thus the sentences of ethics are not meaningful.

Yet it seems odd to deny that sentences which play such a large role in our lives are meaningful; I mean sentences such as

"Killing is wrong," "Democracy is preferable to totalitarianism," and so on. So while the positivists denied descriptive, factual meaning to such sentences, they admitted that they nevertheless had a certain value as expressions of emotion, or as attempts to influence behavior; they had what was called an emotive meaning. The theory that ethical claims have only emotive meaning is known, appropriately enough, as emotivism.

According to emotivism, uttering an ethical sentence such as "Killing is wrong," or "Happiness is good," is not to be construed as describing the world. It is rather like saying "Boo, killing!" and "Hurrah for happiness!" It is giving vent to a feeling. To give vent to a feeling is not, of course, the same as describing the feeling: To say "Killing is wrong" is not, according to the emotivist, the same as saying "I dislike killing." Suppose two men are arguing; one insists that killing is wrong, and the other is intent upon contradicting him. If "Killing is wrong" *meant* "I dislike killing," then it would be either true or false, which the emotivist denies; and to show that it does not mean that, he points out that in the argument we are considering, the proper way for the second man to contradict the one who claims that killing is wrong would be to say "No, you don't dislike killing!" if the ethical sentence were a *description* of a feeling. But we don't contradict ethical claims in that way, and, if the emotivist is right, there isn't any way at all to contradict an ethical claim. To make an ethical claim is not to assert something; it is akin to shouting for joy, or weeping, or snarling. Alfred J. Ayer, who introduced logical positivism into the English-speaking countries in the 1930s with his book *Language, Truth, and Logic*, also introduced in that book the emotive theory in its simplest form:

> It is our business to give an account of "judgments of value" which is both satisfactory in itself and consistent with our general empiricist principles. We shall set ourselves to show that insofar as statements of value are significant, they are ordinary "scientific" statements; and that insofar as they are not scientific, they are not in the literal sense significant, but are simply expressions of emotion which can be neither true nor false.
>
> We begin by admitting that the fundamental ethical concepts are unanalyzable, inasmuch as there is no criterion by which one can test the validity of the judgments in which they occur. So far we are in agreement with the absolutists [like Moore]. But, unlike the absolutists, we are able to give an explanation of this fact about ethical concepts. We say that the reason why they are

unanalyzable is that they are mere pseudo-concepts. The presence of an ethical symbol in a proposition adds nothing to its factual content. Thus if I say to someone, "You acted wrongly in stealing that money," I am not stating anything more than if I had simply said, "You stole that money." In adding that this action is wrong, I am not making any further statement about it. I am simply evincing my moral disapproval of it. It is as if I had said, "You stole that money," in a peculiar tone of horror . . . although our theory of ethics might fairly be said to be radically subjectivist, it differs in a very important respect from the orthodox subjectivist theory. For the orthodox subjectivist does not deny, as we do, that the sentences of a moralizer express genuine propositions.[4]

EMOTIVISM AND PERSUASION

But the meaning of ethical statements is not just expressive; they very obviously have more of a use than that. When I tell my small son that writing in Daddy's books is naughty, he understands (if I am lucky) that I am not simply giving vent to a feeling, that what I say has certain implications for action. If he accepts my admonition, he will cease writing in Daddy's books. The point is that ethical utterances are not only expressive, they are meant to be persuasive as well. It is because of the persuasive element that there can be ethical disagreement. For my son to disagree that such activity is naughty is for him to refuse to act in the way in which I am encouraging him to act.

This persuasive aspect of ethical utterances is not only consistent with emotivism, emotivism requires some such addition to explain the possibility of ethical disagreement, and to explain the connection between ethics and action. The bare expressive theory of ethics is not adequate to what are generally agreed to be the facts surrounding ethical discussion. Let us take under consideration, then, an expanded emotivist theory which admits the persuasive use of ethical statements.

This more complete emotivist theory is in line with the original aim of the empiricist: If ethical utterances are expressive and persuasive, but not ultimately factual or descriptive, then there is no need to explain how ethical terms might be reduced

---

4. Alfred J. Ayer, *Language, Truth and Logic* (London: Gollancz, 1936), pp. 102–3.

to observation terms. Remember that it was generally conceded that such a reduction would be impossible (Moore's thesis).

But the expanded emotive theory, as it stands, has important flaws. In the first place, the point in uttering an ethical statement is certainly not always to persuade someone to take a certain course of action. I might carry on an ethical discussion with someone, for example, whom I can expect to agree with me in every detail, and who is already disposed to act in ways I find acceptable; in such cases I am not likely to be trying to persuade anyone to do anything. In fact, it can be argued that persuasion—goading to action—is very rarely the *point* of ethical discussion; neither is expression of feelings the point of such discussion. Certainly I might persuade someone, and I might give vent to my feelings *in the course* of an ethical discussion, but so might I persuade someone, and give vent to my feeling in the course of giving the time of day—for example, when I say to friends who have overstayed, "Look, it's two o'clock in the morning." That does not mean that my time-of-day utterance has emotive meaning only.

Any utterance can be used to persuade, to give vent to feelings, but talk about the meaning of an utterance is different from talk about its persuasiveness or expressiveness. In fact, it seems to be precisely because of the information they convey that certain sentences have the persuasive or expressive function they do. This does not mean that ethical sentences must be primarily conveyors of information to be meaningful at all; it does suggest that persuasiveness and expressiveness are probably incidental to whatever it is for which ethical sentences *are* primarily used.

The distinction to be made here is the distinction between what J. L. Austin called the *illocutionary* force of an utterance, and what he called the *perlocutionary* force.[5] The illocutionary force of an utterance depends on what can be done *in* issuing that utterance, according to commonly accepted rules governing such utterances. In uttering a promise, reciting the marriage vows, hanging a No-Trespass sign, describing one's birthplace, what is being done is clear enough: One is making a promise, getting married, warning off trespassers, telling about a location. Whether any of the utterances involved arouse any emotions, or cause any action, that is not part of the illocutionary force of the utterances. Whether or not those emotions had been aroused,

---

5. J. L. Austin discusses this distinction in his *How to Do Things with Words* (Oxford: Clarendon Pr., 1962), pp. 99–131.

or those actions caused, the utterances involved could still be said to have done their jobs. But a trespass sign that warned no one, a description that told nothing about the place—these are examples of utterances that are failures as illocutionary acts.

On the other hand, if any of these utterances were able to arouse someone's emotion, or to cause some kind of action, then they had perlocutionary force; something could be accomplished *by means* of them. If I hang a No-Trespass sign to shame my neighbors, what I am doing in hanging the sign is still warning off trespassers, but what I am doing *by means of* that action is shaming my neighbors. So shaming my neighbors would be part of the perlocutionary force of the sign. Similarly, if I utter the marriage vows, my aim might be to thereby come into a fortune, but the illocutionary force of the wedding vows has to do with getting married; the perlocutionary force they have, might have to do with my coming into a fortune.

Now the emotivists thought that they had said what ethical statements were used for, when they described the expressive and persuasive functions that ethical language has. But clearly that is like supposing that we could tell what the language of warnings is used for when we say that so-and-so used it to shame his neighbors, and that others have used it in similar ways. The use that we have assigned to the language of warnings is to warn. It is only because it has that use that it can be used in other, almost incidental ways. (Part of the perlocutionary force hanging a trespass sign can have that is not so incidental is to keep people off my property! Nevertheless even that can be distinguished from the illocutionary force, since I may use such a sign precisely to entice people of a certain sort onto my land.)

We may express feelings, and persuade others, by means of ethical utterances, but we can use ethical language in that way because of its illocutionary force. The discussion of ethical language should concern itself primarily with the illocutionary force, whatever that might be. How language of any sort, and not just ethical language, can be used to express or arouse emotion, or persuade to action is perhaps more properly a question for psychology than for philosophy.

To ask what it is that we do in saying that something is wrong (a question that might arise if we agree with the emotivists that what we are *not* doing is describing some state of affairs), is to ask for the illocutionary force. The perlocutionary force, while not totally independent of the illocutionary, is something else entirely. It is something that a particular act of utterance can have in virtue of its illocutionary force, and what we know about the behavior of people when faced with that illocutionary force. In the right circumstances, a locution might have any perlocutionary force you can imagine.

But if the illocutionary force of ethical discourse is not persuasion or expression or the conveying of information, then what is it? The suggestion has been that it is to commend, to suggest, to guide. The emotivists had thought that it was to express feeling and to goad to action. The difference between guiding and goading is simple enough. We can goad someone along a road with a cattle prod, but we cannot goad him with signposts, although if he so chooses, he can be guided by the signposts. The suggestion being made here is that ethical discourse resembles the use of signposts rather than the use of prods.[6]

THE DESCRIPTIVE ELEMENT IN ETHICAL LANGUAGE

But is it true that ethical sentences convey no information? Can it be that some action is right, some state of affairs good, independently of all the facts? The separation of ethics from factual discourse cannot be so complete that someone who tells us that such-and-such is good tells us nothing at all about its other attributes. If such a complete separation were possible, then this situation would also be possible: Two states of affairs might resemble one another in every respect except one, namely, that one was good, and the other not good. Such a situation seems impossible. Surely if two states of affairs resemble each other in every nonethical respect, then if one is good, the other must be good as well. To go further than that, it seems reasonable to say even that ethical claims must be based on certain observable characteristics of things and states of affairs. We can agree with Moore that those observable characteristics cannot be part of the *meaning* of the ethical claim (or in other language, that it is not a primary function of ethical language to convey information about those characteristics); yet we must also agree that the ethical claims are associated with those char-

---

6. This point is made in W. D. Falk's "Goading and Guiding," reprinted in *Readings in the Problems of Ethics*, ed. by Rosalind Ekman (New York: Scribner, 1965).

acteristics in a way that is not mere happenstance—that they are ncessarily associated with them in some way.

If X, Y, and Z are characteristics that we take to be associated with all and only good states of affairs, then in telling someone that state of affairs *p* is good, we are not only directing his action toward *p*, we are telling him something from which he may reasonably conclude that *p* has characteristics X, Y, and Z. But now, what sort of statement is the statement that any state of affairs that has X, Y, and Z is good? Moore would say that the "natural" properties X, Y, and Z are not part of the meaning of "good"; consequently, the statement cannot be analytic, if Moore is right—as I think he must be. Neither is the statement empirically verifiable; we do not learn through observation that goodness is associated with X, Y, and Z. Thus for the empiricist, for whom all meaningful propositions are either analytic or empirically verifiable, all that remains is to deny that any information at all is conveyed in such ultimate utterances. Such utterances must be similar in nature to commands. Furthermore, they are commands of a particular ultimate sort, not susceptible to any justification. The relation of goodness to X, Y, and Z resolves itself entirely into a decision that I might make; it cannot be based on any further attributes that X, Y, and Z might involve.

We seem to be working our way toward a theory that resembles emotivism in denying that the primary function of ethical language is to describe; that disagrees with emotivism about the primary function of ethical language, which it takes to be commending and guiding much as we do in giving commands, rather than expression and persuasion; that maintains a connection between ethical language and descriptive language; and which holds that connection to be based on a decision we make. A proponent of a similar theory is R. M. Hare.[7] For Hare, ethical statements do resemble prescriptions or commands, and as such they are based, in the end, not on any facts in the world about us, but on decisions that we make. His position is supported by a careful discussion of the ways in which we do use the language of ethics.

It is possible to distinguish, among disagreements over what is right and what is not, disagreements of fact from disagree-

---

7. For Hare's view, *see* his *Language of Morals* (Oxford: Clarendon Pr., 1950). For a discussion, *see* George Kerner's *Revolution in Ethical Theory* (London: Oxford Univ. Pr., 1966).

ments of value. Suppose that you and I disagree about what is the right course of action in a particular case. It may be that we simply disagree as to what the facts of the case are, so that a little investigation might settle the thing; if we knew what the facts were, then, agreeing essentially about what is right and what is not, we might come to some agreement. But it might also be the case that each of us knows perfectly well what the facts are; we very simply disagree about what things are right and what things are wrong. In this case, no amount of investigation would resolve our difference; it is based on a disagreement of value.

Since ultimately our ethical positions cannot be changed by knowledge of the facts, those positions cannot be based on or derived from facts. Thus Hare, and the emotivists too, and Moore before them, seem to be right, finally, on the separation of fact and value. Where Hare differs from the emotivists is, in the first place, in his characterization of ethical utterances as prescriptive, not expressive or persuasive. If ethical statements are ultimately prescriptions, then either such prescriptions are rooted in the nature of man, or they are freely chosen. But the possibility of ultimate disagreement rules out such a rooting in a human nature. Thus they must be decisions, freely chosen. All ethics is thus a matter of choice, within limits set by the nature of ethics itself.

RETURN TO NATURALISM

Not everyone has been willing, of course, to agree that ethics is independent of facts. On the side of the so-called naturalists, who believe that ethics can be derived from the facts, J. R. Searle argues in this way. Whether or not someone utters the words "I promise to return this" is a question of fact, and what the circumstances are that surround the utterance (whether he was under compulsion to utter it, whether he was being frivolous) is also a question of fact. But if someone in the appropriate circumstances utters the words "I promise to return this," then he has promised to return it. So it is a factual question whether someone has made a promise. But whoever has made a promise has obligated himself in some way. So sometimes at least it can be factually determined that someone has obligated himself. From obligating oneself it follows that one is obligated, and thus that one *ought* to act in a certain way.[8]

Thus that one ought to act in a certain way follows from certain facts about utterances and circumstances; and so ethical statements can be derived from factual statements, and the alleged gap between fact and value does not exist. Moore was wrong, say the naturalists, and so were the emotivists and prescriptivists.

To see whether Searle has in fact derived an ethical statement from a factual one, let's set the argument out a little more clearly:

> PREMISE: Under suitable conditions Jones uttered the words "I promise to pay Smith five dollars."
>
> CONCLUSION: Therefore Jones ought to pay Smith five dollars.

The premise is factual, the conclusion is ethical. If the argument is valid, Searle has succeeded in deriving an ethical conclusion from factual premises. But the argument as it stands is too spare; it is not clear that the conclusion does follow from the premises. We need to add more premises, but we cannot add any ethical premises, since our object is to derive, if possible, an ethical conclusion from entirely factual premises.

We can fill out the argument in roughly this way:

> PREMISE 1: Under suitable conditions Jones uttered the words "I promise to pay Smith five dollars."
>
> PREMISE 2: If anyone utters, under suitable conditions, the words, "I promise to pay Smith five dollars," then he has promised to pay Smith five dollars.
>
> PREMISE 3: If anyone has promised to pay Smith five dollars, then he has placed himself under an obligation to pay Smith five dollars.

8. *See* Searle's "How to Derive 'Ought' from 'Is'," in Philippa Foot, ed., *Theories of Ethics* (London: Oxford Univ. Pr., 1967).

PREMISE 4: If anyone has placed himself under
an obligation to pay Smith five dollars,
then he ought to pay Smith five dollars.

CONCLUSION: Therefore Jones ought to pay Smith
five dollars.

Now this argument, as it stands, seems to be valid. From premises 2 through 4, by applying the priniciple that from *If A then B* and *if B then C* we may infer *If A then C*, we get the conclusion that

If anyone, under suitable conditions, utters
the words "I promise to pay Smith five dollars,"
then he ought to pay Smith five dollars.

And from that conclusion and premise 1, the conclusion that Jones ought to pay Smith five dollars follows.

Since the argument, as expanded, does seem to be valid, the only thing left to the nonnaturalist to question is whether each of the four premises is factual and not ethical. If they are all factual, and not ethical, then Searle will indeed have succeeded in deriving an ethical conclusion from factual premises by means of a valid argument. Premise 1 does not seem to be ethical; the conditions under which something was uttered are a matter of fact. The other premises, Searle insists, are simple tautologies: For example, it is analytically true that whoever utters a promise sentence in certain circumstances is making a promise—that's what we mean by "making a promise," after all.

Moore might have objected here that it cannot be analytic that whoever makes a promise is under obligation to keep it; it is always an open question, and not absurd to ask, whether one is under obligation to keep one's promises. And in fact there do seem to be times when one has no obligation to keep his promise. Thus premise 3, if Moore was right, is not analytic.

Prescriptivists, on the other hand, might object that such an approach as Searle's, if extended to ethics in general (and it would not be of any interest unless it could be extended to cover all of ethics) would ask us to ignore the possibility of fundamental ethical disagreement. For if ethical judgments follow from the facts, no one who knew the facts and understood the words involved could disagree about what is right and what is wrong. Yet, as we have seen, it does sometimes seem that men who know the facts and agree on the use of words disagree on what is right and what is wrong. And if that is so, then ethical judgments do not follow from facts.

Searle answers the first objection in this way: Although under certain circumstances we do not have to keep our promises, that does not prove that we were not originally under any obligation. And if we were originally under no obligation, that simply shows that the conditions were not fulfilled for making a promise. The fact remains that if the conditions are right, Jones has placed himself under an obligation.

The second objection is more fundamental, and can be raised in general against the attempt to derive ethical statements from factual statements. The answer to it might be this: Where there seems to be an ethical disagreement that is not a disagreement of fact, it is a disagreement about the way words are used, about what follows from what. One of the disputants may mistakenly reject one of the tautological premises 2, 3, or 4 in Searle's argument, for example. You and I might disagree about whether "bachelor" means "unmarried male" and therefore disagree about whether from "He is a bachelor" we can infer "He is a male." But the fact of our disagreement doesn't, all by itself, show that the inference can't be made. It can. The problem is simply that one of us doesn't understand how the words involved are used.

And so in ethics, the naturalist might argue, the fact that we disagree about what ethical conclusion follows from the facts doesn't show that *no* ethical conclusion follows from the facts. Thus the objection has no force.

The naturalist has chosen to avoid the issue by arguing against the possibility of fundamental ethical difference. About this two things may be said: First, even if that point is correct, it does not establish that ethical conclusions can be derived from the facts; and second, it seems clear that ethical disagreements which are neither disagreements about the facts nor disagreements about the meaning of words are certainly possible—to suppose otherwise is to suppose that the worst criminals of history were ignorant either of the facts or of the meanings of words, if they claimed their actions were right.[9]

---

9. Naturalism is discussed in most books on contemporary ethical theory; *see* G. J. Warnock's *Contemporary Moral Philosophy* (London: Macmillan, 1967).

UTILITARIANISM AND JUSTICE

At the beginning of this chapter I declared that utilitarianism is the most widely accepted ethical theory in analytic philosophy, and I said that there were two main problems facing a utilitarianism such as the one advocated by Mill. The first was the problem of saying just what sort of claim "Happiness is good" is. We have up till now been discussing various answers to that question; the discussion has taken us through Moore's criticism of naturalism, the emotive theory, prescriptivism, and back to naturalism. It has been a discussion of what is called metaethics: it has concerned the meaning of ethical terms, and the status of ethical principles, without presupposing that any particular ethical principle is correct. This latter question—which ethical principle is correct—we will take up now in trying to answer the second problem facing utilitarianism: Is utilitarianism, as a theory, adequate to what we know to be right and wrong? Such questions, questions about specific ethical standards, are questions of normative ethics; they are questions about what is right, and not about the meanings of terms. Whether there is any connection between normative and metaethics, whether an answer to "Which principle is correct?" follows from an answer to "What is the meaning of 'good'?" is something we will not try to answer.

The great obstacle to the utilitarian principle—that action is right which produces the greatest happiness for the greatest number—is the problem of justice. If, as utilitarianism suggests, there is one principle of ethics, from which all others follow, then one of the principles that should follow from that supreme principle is the principle of justice—that we should treat all men fairly, or, to put it another way, that we should not treat two men differently unless there is some relevant difference between them.

But the principle of justice does not follow from the principle of utility. We may greatly increase the happiness of the greatest number by being unfair. Imagine the following case: A certain society is on the brink of anarchy because the police have seemed incapable of solving a particularly heinous sort of crime; people are losing faith in the structure of their society and the mechanism of its law enforcement. The chief of police, satisfied that this sort of crime will probably never be repeated in any case, takes it upon himself to arrest a stranger in the community.

With the complicity of the judges involved, the man is found guilty of the crime. He is hanged. The confidence of the people is restored; the community is returned to its happy condition.

According to the letter of utilitarianism, the action of the officials involved was right. The great relief and happiness of the people is offset only by the short-lived terror of the innocent man; and with sufficient technical knowledge the man could have been kept tranquil throughout his trial and right up to his execution. There is only happiness to consider, then; surely the action of the chief was right.

But of course the action was not right; it was unjust, and we could never condone punishment of the innocent. Even if we did, however, the point has been made. The principle of utility does not entail the principle of justice, since the principle of utility sometimes entails that we must be unjust.

If we accept the argument on its face, there are two courses open to us if we want to maintain the principle of utility. We may admit that there must be at least two main principles of ethics, utility and justice, with one or the other taking precedence in time of dispute. That move would be a denial of simple utilitarianism. The other move would be to insist that although such cases are rare, in the case described the injustice would in fact be right. I don't think this last move would work; the circumstances imagined could be made bizarre; utilitarianism could be made to entail judgments whose incorrectness is perfectly clear. Consider, instead of a case of punishing the innocent, slavery in a society that condones it; consider any oppression of a minority group for the enrichment of the many. It would not be too difficult to imagine an example of what was by general agreement a great wrong, and yet was called right by the principle of utility. It would seem that the only course left open is to accept the two-principle compromise. (We could, of course, look into the merit of the ethical theory whose single principle was the principle of justice. There are severe difficulties with a theory in which justice is not mitigated with utility. Justice by itself tends to be barren; it would condone killing an innocent man—as long as we killed all innocent men!)

But there may be another way out for utilitarianism, a way that enables the utilitarian to reject the argument about the innocent man. It goes like this: The argument depends upon a failure to distinguish between *particular actions* and *rules*. Certainly, if utilitarianism were taken to be the principle that every individual act is to be tested on the basis of its consequences, then the argument against it is relevant. An ethical theory that takes the principle in that way could be called an *act-utilitarian* theory. But that is the wrong way to take the principle. Utilitarianism should be identified with the more sophisticated principle which claims that it is rules that are to be tested against the consequences of adhering to those rules. That principle is the principle of *rule-utilitarianism*.[10] Against this form of utilitarianism, according to this way out of the difficulty, the argument is not relevant. For although in the particular case before him the chief of police could effect more happiness by punishing an innocent man, certainly in the long run a rule which allowed the police to persecute the innocent would create a great deal of unhappiness. It would eventually undermine the confidence of the people, and create a state of fear. Thus the chief's action is wrong, since it is in accord with a rule that is wrong—the consequences of obeying the rule would be worse than the consequences of not obeying it. Similarly *any* rule that directed men to act against justice would eventually create more unhappiness; and so, indirectly, the principle of justice *is* entailed by the principle of utility, as long as the principle of utility is understood as a principle of rule- rather than act-utility.

Unfortunately, it would seem that the same sort of objection can be raised against rule-utilitarianism as the case of the innocent man raised against act-utilitarianism. For certainly a rule could be imagined that would ensure the happiness of the majority at the expense of the suffering of a few who did not deserve to suffer. And if such a rule were possible, then rule-utilitarianism would tell us that actions in accordance with that rule are right. Consequently, rule-utilitarianism seems also to be mistaken. The question is whether any further refinement of utilitarianism would be sufficient to overcome the objections.

SUGGESTIONS FOR FURTHER READING

There are a number of standard introductions to the study of ethics. William Frankena's *Ethics*, in the Foundations of Philosophy series (Englewood Cliffs, N.J.: Prentice-Hall, 1963; a new

10. The issue of act- versus rule-utilitarianism is developed in the essays collected by Michael Bayles in *Contemporary Utilitarianism* (Garden City, N.Y.: Doubleday, 1968).

edition is forthcoming), emphasizes normative ethics, but devotes a chapter to metaethics. It is a good book with which to begin the study of ethics. Richard B. Brandt's *Ethical Theory* (Englewood Cliffs, N.J.: Prentice-Hall, 1959) is also a fairly standard introduction; it is much more comprehensive than Frankena's book. There are several books devoted mainly to metaethics, and most of them have the same format. The following books, for example, all trace the development of metaethics through intuitionism, emotivism, prescriptivism, and naturalism, in pretty much that order: G. J. Warnock's *Contemporary Moral Philosophy* (London: Macmillan, 1967); W. D. Hudson's *Modern Moral Philosophy* (Garden City, N.Y.: Doubleday, 1970); and George Kerner's *Revolution in Ethical Theory* (London: Oxford Univ. Pr., 1966).

There are also a number of standard anthologies of readings in ethics, for example: Richard B. Brandt (ed.), *Value and Obligation* (New York: Harcourt, 1961); P. W. Taylor (ed.), *The Moral Judgment* (Englewood Cliffs, N.J.: Prentice-Hall, 1963); Wilfrid S. Sellars and John Hospers (eds.), *Readings in Ethical Theory* (New York: Appleton, 1970)—with readings in metaethics through 1952. There are also a number of anthologies that have not had time to become standard, but which are very useful, for example: Philippa Foot (ed.), *Theories of Ethics* (London: Oxford Univ. Pr., 1967); Gerald Dworkin and J. J. Thomson (eds.), *Ethics* (New York: Harper, 1968); and Michael Bayles (ed.), *Contemporary Utilitarianism* (Garden City, N.Y.: Doubleday, 1968), which contains most of the important recent articles on utilitarianism.

Recent discussion in ethical theory began with G. E. Moore's *Principia Ethica* (Cambridge: Cambridge Univ. Pr., 1903); Moore called himself an intuitionist, by which he seems to have meant only that he considered good to be indefinable. The best case for emotivism is probably made in Charles Stevenson's *Ethics and Language* (New Haven: Yale Univ. Pr., 1943); a section of Alfred J. Ayer's *Language, Truth, and Logic* (London: Gollancz, 1936) is also devoted to emotivism. More recent books on ethical theory are R. M. Hare's *Language of Morals* (Oxford: Clarendon Pr., 1950) and his *Freedom and Reason* (Oxford: Clarendon Pr., 1963); Stephen E. Toulmin's *An Examination of the Place of Reason in Ethics* (Cambridge: Cambridge Univ. Pr., 1950); Kurt Baier's *Moral Point of View* (Ithaca, N.Y.: Cornell Univ. Pr., 1958); and P. H. Nowell-Smith's *Ethics* (London: Penguin, 1954). Among recent books on utilitarianism, there is J. J. C.

Smart's *Outline of a System of Utilitarian Ethics* (Melbourne: Melbourne Univ. Pr., 1961).

From among the important recent papers on both normative and metaethics, we include only a few. William Frankena's "The Naturalistic Fallacy" is an important discussion of Moore's argument against naturalism, reprinted in Sellars and Hospers. On the dispute between prescriptivism and naturalism, are John Searle's "How to Derive 'Ought' from 'Is'," and a reply by R. M. Hare, "The Promising Game," both reprinted in Philippa Foot's anthology. Utilitarianism seems unable to account for the praiseworthiness of actions that are above and beyond the call of duty; see J. O. Urmson's "Saints and Heroes" (in *Essays in Moral Philosophy*, ed. by A. I. Melden [Seattle: Univ. of Washington Pr., 1958]). On the same point, see papers by Joel Feinberg and Roderick M. Chisholm in the Dworkin and Thomson anthology. And finally, all of the articles reprinted in the Bayles collection are to be recommended; one of the most important papers to be found there is John Rawls's "Two Concepts of Rules."

For the reader who would like to approach the study of ethics systematically, it would be good to begin with John Stuart Mill's *Utilitarianism*; and then to read Moore's *Principia Ethica*; Stevenson's *Ethics and Language*; Hare's *Language of Morals*; and the papers in the Bayles volume.

Most of *The Encyclopedia of Philosophy* (ed. by Paul Edwards [New York: Macmillan, 1967]) articles in this area are very helpful; see especially "The Emotive Theory of Ethics" and "Epistemology and Ethics," by Richard B. Brandt, and "Ethics —Problems of," by Kai Nielsen.

John Rawls's *A Theory of Justice* (Cambridge, Mass.: Harvard Univ. Pr., 1971) is widely considered to be one of the most important contributions to ethics by an analytic philosopher in many years. In it Rawls develops an alternative to the utilitarian view of justice, an alternative situated in the social contract tradition. While the importance of this book would be hard to exaggerate, it should be emphasized that Rawls is not offering us a complete theory of ethics, but rather (just as the title indicates) a theory of social justice.

CHAPTER 6

LOGIC
AND
ANALYTIC
PHILOSOPHY

A good deal of what we have been discussing up to now has had to do with meaning—the meaning of ethical terms, the meaning of perceptual claims, the meaning of statements about mental activity; whether some sorts of statements are meaningless; and so on. With the problem of empiricism in mind, we have asked whether ethical claims can be analyzed into claims about observable properties, whether they are logical truths, or whether they are meaningless. We have asked the same about perceptual claims, and about psychological claims. In each case we seem forced to the conclusion that some statements are neither meaningless, nor logical, nor analyzable into simple, empirical statements.

To the extent that our discussion has been a discussion of meaning, the problems we have been dealing with fall under the general heading of logic, or of what is sometimes called the philosophy of logic. In this chapter we bring together some of the important conclusions we have reached, and discuss their implications for the philosophy of logic. We began with a discussion of logic and meaning, and it seems appropriate to end with a discussion of logic and meaning.

THE PRINCIPLE
OF EXTENSIONALITY

Frege believed that the theory of meaning should have two parts, a theory of the *sense* or connotation, sometimes called the intension, of expressions, and a theory of the *reference* or denotation, sometimes called the extension, of expressions.[1] In plain circumstances the reference of a name is the thing it refers to and its sense is the concept it expresses. Two names may name or refer to the same thing without having the same sense. For example, if lines A, B, and C all intersect at a certain point *p*, then the point denoted by "the intersection of A and B" is the same as the point denoted by "the intersection of B and C," namely *p*. But even though those expressions have the same reference they do not have the same sense; their senses are different, and that is why the sentence "The intersection of A and B is the same point as the intersection of B and C" is not trivially true, but rather informative; if the senses were the same, then the sentence would be trivially true. This sort of reasoning underlies the distinction between sense and reference, connotation and denotation, intension and extension.

Similarly the sense of a sentence is the proposition that it expresses; its reference is either truth or falsity—truth if it is true, falsity if it is false. Frege decided that the reference of sentences should be truth or falsity and not, say, the propositions the sentences express because he believed that the reference of a complex expression—like a sentence—was a function of the reference of the parts; thus, the reference of a sentence should not change when of two terms having the same reference one was replaced by the other in that sentence. But such a replacement could change the proposition expressed, so the proposition cannot be the reference of the sentence. What would remain unchanged would be the truth-value involved (though, as we will see, there are important exceptions that must be ac-

1. Gottlob Frege, "On Sense and Denotation," in Herbert Feigl and Wilfrid S. Sellars, *Readings in Philosophical Analysis* (New York: Appleton, 1949).

counted for). Frege felt that he was compelled to conclude that the reference of a sentence is its truth-value.[2] Here is the sort of example we are dealing with: Bertrand Russell is the best-known twentieth-century analytic philosopher. Consequently we should be able to exchange "Bertrand Russell" for "the best-known twentieth-century analytic philosopher," which has the same reference, in any sentence without changing the reference of that sentence. But consider the change from

> The best-known twentieth-century analytic philosopher was a philosopher

to

> Bertrand Russell was a philosopher.

It is easily shown that these two sentences express different propositions: A person might know that one is true, and yet believe the other false, which could not be the case if they expressed the same proposition. What remains unchanged is the truth-value; consequently of the two—proposition and truth-value—only the truth-value could be considered the reference of the sentence.

A two-level theory of meaning might be filled out like this:

EXPRESSION:	name	predicate	sentence
SENSE:	concept	property	proposition
REFERENCE:	thing	the class of things having that property	truth-value

In our discussion of the identity theory in chapter 4, we were discussing a theory that claimed that while the *senses* of mental expressions are different from the *senses* of any physical expressions, nevertheless the *references* were in some cases the same. In the following chapter we looked into an argument that said in effect that although the reference of the word "happy" might be exactly the same set of states of affairs that the word "good" refers to, nevertheless the two words cannot "mean" the same; that is, their senses must be different. Thus the distinction between sense and reference can be a useful one to make.

That we make such a distinction, however, and adopt such a two-level theory of meaning, seems to require that we at least feel comfortable talking about concepts, properties and propositions. Not all philosophers do. Quine's argument against the

2. Ibid., pp. 89–92.

notion of analyticity that we looked at in chapter 3 was really directed against the idea of an intensional level of meaning; if it is not clearly meaningful to talk about two expressions having the same sense (as the notion of analyticity requires), then perhaps it is not meaningful, nor any longer very useful, to talk about senses, or connotation, or intensions at all.

It isn't too difficult to understand the desire to avoid talking about intensional entities—concepts, properties, propositions, states of affairs—if at all possible. We can see what someone has in mind when he says that there are tables and chairs. We know what tables and chairs are; we can count them, if necessary; we can tell them apart. But if someone were to insist that there are propositions—not just in a manner of speaking, but *really*— what is it that he would be saying? How would he expect things to be different if there were no propositions? Propositions would be strange things to have to acknowledge. How do you tell when you are faced with a proposition? And how do you tell one proposition from two? Philosophers have tried to avoid such unmanageable entities whenever possible. Those to whom intensional entities remain unwelcome are by and large convinced that we can do without them; and their opponents, those who hold for such intensional entities, do not do so out of a sentimental attachment to such things, but rather because of the conviction that we are required, by this fact or that, to admit their existence. Consider, for example, Frege's reasons for supposing that there are such intensional entities.

Frege adopted the two-level approach because it enabled him to explain certain apparent divergencies from the principle of extensionality. That principle says, in one of its versions:

> Two expressions referring to the same thing
> can be substituted one for the other in any
> sentence without changing the truth-value
> of the sentence.

For example, "Augustus," having the same reference, can be substituted for "the first emperor of Rome" in

> The adopted son of Julius Caesar was the
> first emperor of Rome

without changing the truth-value of that sentence.

But apparently the principle fails in belief-sentences, and in other sorts of sentences as well. "Augustus" and "the first emperor of Rome" do refer to the same individual; yet they are not interchangeable in belief-sentences. We have had occasion to allude to this difficulty elsewhere. Consider the following two sentences:

> John believes that Augustus was the
> adopted son of Julius Caesar.

> John believes that the first emperor of
> Rome was the adopted son of Julius Caesar.

One of those sentences might quite well be true while the other is false. Imagine, for example, that John does not know that Augustus was the first emperor of Rome, even though he knows that Augustus was the adopted son of Julius; suppose he thought mistakenly that Julius was the first emperor. Then the first of the sentences above would be true, and the second false. Here we seem to have a counterexample to the principle of extensionality: A sentence in which two expressions referring to the same thing cannot be interchanged without changing the truth-value of the sentence.

Frege's two levels of meaning give him a way to save the principle; the two levels cannot change the facts, but they give a way for showing that the principle is consistent with the facts. The move to be made is this: Words have a certain reference when used in simple sentences, outside of the context of belief, indirect quotation, or other similar contexts. In simple sentences "Augustus" and "the first emperor of Rome" have the same reference; that is why they can be substituted one for the other in simple sentences. But in a special context like belief, the reference of those expressions changes; in such contexts such expressions *refer* to what used to be their *sense*.[3] In the sentence

> John believes that Augustus was the
> adopted son of Julius Caesar

the expression "Augustus" does not refer to the individual Augustus; rather it refers to the concept of Augustus. And that is why the expression "the first emperor of Rome" cannot be substituted for it in that sentence. Although both expressions have the same reference in ordinary contexts, in these so-called indirect contexts like belief one of them refers to the concept of Augustus (which in ordinary contexts was its sense) and the other refers to the concept of the first emperor of Rome; and

---

3. Ibid., pp. 92 ff.

since those two concepts are not the same, the expressions do not, in indirect contexts, refer to the same thing. And so they cannot be substituted one for the other in indirect contexts. And thus the fact that they cannot be substituted for one another is consistent with the principle of extensionality, and not a counter-example to it.

In every context, then, we can interchange words that refer to the same thing one for the other, but we must keep in mind that expressions change their reference in certain contexts; in those contexts they refer to what they in ordinary contexts connote. We could, in the sentence above, substitute for "Augustus" any other expression which in indirect contexts referred to the concept of Augustus.

Why should anyone be so concerned to save the principle of extensionality? Why go to all the bother? Why not simply give up the principle? A. N. Prior, for example, in *Objects of Thought*[4] makes that suggestion. It is tempting to believe that one of the reasons philosophers have struggled so valiantly to save the principle is their conviction that the principle of extensionality is equivalent to another priniciple, which we may call the principle of the indiscernibility of identicals, which says that

$$(x)(y)(x=y \supset (F)(Fx \equiv Fy)),$$

if you happen to remember your symbolism; if you don't, it says that for any x and y, x is the same individual as y only if x and y have all the same properties. This principle cannot be false. Try to imagine a counterexample. Suppose that x is y, yet x has some property y doesn't. It cannot be done. Notice how this principle resembles the principle of extensionality; it may be that because of this similarity between the two principles those who were trying to save the principle of extensionality had it confused with the indiscernibility of identicals. They were right in thinking that the indiscernibility of identicals couldn't be false; they were wrong in thinking that principle is the same as the principle of extensionality.[5]

4. Arthur N. Prior, *Objects of Thought* (Oxford: Clarendon Pr., 1971).
5. Russell, if I am not mistaken, makes this confusion very explicitly in "On Denoting," in his *Logic and Knowledge* (London: Allen & Unwin, 1956); he says there "If *a* is identical with *b*, whatever is true of the one is true of the other, and either may be substituted for the other in any proposition without altering the truth value of a proposition" (p. 47).

The two principles are not the same. What is required to go from one to the other is the supposition that every context of a name expresses a property; that "John believes that ——— was the adopted son of Julius Caesar," for example, expresses a property that applies to whatever "Augustus" happens to refer to. But there is no reason to suppose that every context of a name expresses a property.[6] If we allow that not every context expresses a property, then we can separate the two principles; and we can deny extensionality without denying the indiscernibility of identicals. To deny extensionality is not to deny that expressions have both a sense and a reference, but it does do away with a problem that that distinction was needed to solve.

An alternative to Frege's two-level theory of meaning is a one-level theory that would identify the theory of meaning with the theory of reference—a theory that tries to show that the meaning of a word is simply its reference. The viability of such a theory depends pretty much on what we will allow among the referents of words, what we will countenance in our world. A theory which countenances only individual objects, for example, will not do. Although such a sentence as "The average man is 5'11" " can be translated into a (very long) conjunction of sentences about individual men—"John Smith is 5'8" and George Matczak is 6'1" and . . ."—that does not show that all our sentences are about individual objects. For there are some sentences that cannot be translated into sentences about individuals; one of them is

There are virtues that nobody has.

The sentence "Honesty is a virtue that nobody has" can be translated into the conjunction "John Smith is not honest and George Matczak is not honest and . . ." and so might be construed as being about individual men. But there is no similar way to translate "There are virtues that no one has"; the translation "There is a virtue that John Smith doesn't have and that George Matczak doesn't have and . . ." is not just about individual men but about a virtue, and so about a property, since virtues are properties. And so, it may be argued, even if we choose the one-level theory of meaning, we must admit in that one-level, properties as well as individual objects. Russell, as an atomist, held

---

6. *See* the second paragraph below for one alternative.

a one-level theory of meaning; and at different times he seems to have held that the referents of expressions included individuals and concepts, concepts alone, and events alone.[7] Moore, in one early paper at least, felt the world was made up of concepts.[8] It has been suggested that individuals and classes are sufficient to account for the theory of meaning of the language of science; add to this the claim that everything that can be said about the world can be said in the language of science, and we have roughly the position of Quine.[9]

Certainly if we admit not only individuals but also properties and states of affairs the one-level theory of meaning will be adequate. A sentence like

> John believes that Augustus was the
> adopted son of Julius Caesar

can be seen to express a relation between an individual and a state of affairs, between John and Augustus-being-the-adopted-son-of-Julius Caesar. And if we add the stipulation that Augustus-being-the-adopted-son-of-Julius Caesar is not the same state of affairs as the-first-emperor-of-Rome-being-the-adopted-son-of-Julius Caesar, we can account for the fact that John might believe one of them to hold and not believe the other to hold. But although individuals, properties, and states of affairs may be adequate it is not clear that all three are necessary. We can say this much; those who turned to a one-level theory of meaning because of their distaste for the intensional entities of Frege's theory— the concepts, properties, and propositions—may find themselves forced to admit those or similar entities at the level of reference. In section 4 of this chapter, the section on ontological commitment, we will look further into these issues.

THE VERIFIABILITY
CRITERION

The verifiability criterion was supposed, by the positivists, to measure the limits of meaningfulness. Not only is it required of

7. Individuals and concepts in *The Problems of Philosophy* (London: Oxford Univ. Pr., and New York: Henry Holt, 1912), concepts earlier than that, and events afterwards.

8. G. E. Moore, "On the Nature of Judgment," *Mind* 14 (1899): 176–93.

9. W. V. O. Quine's position seems to have evolved some; he seems more tolerant in *Philosophy of Logic* (Englewood Cliffs, N.J.: Prentice-Hall, 1970).

us to give a positive theory of meaning, it is required of us to say where meaning stops. It was by means of such a limit that the Vienna Circle proposed, as we have seen, to deal with the sentences of metaphysics that had troubled philosophers for so long. Any nonlogical statement, decreed the Circle, which is not at least in principle verifiable is not meaningful. Here is the basis for the emotive theory of ethics; ethical statements are not meaningful, for how would you go about verifying them? Here is the impetus to phenomenalism; if the relation of appearances to reality is not purely logical, how could claims about the relation be verified? And behaviorism—if claims about mental events are not just about behavior, how could they be verified? So they are just about behavior, or else meaningless. Much of traditional metaphysics is just thrown out. Statements about God, personal survival, and so on, are unverifiable and meaningless—except for whatever emotive content they may have. But in any case they say nothing about the world.

And so the verifiability criterion attempted to define the limits of meaningfulness. But the criterion had certain flaws, in addition to the apparent failure of phenomenalism, behaviorism, and the emotive theory. For one thing, the criterion itself could not be verified and was not a logical truth; so according to it, it was itself meaningless. For another thing, it excluded from the arena of meaningfulness some sentences that were obviously meaningful, and allowed as meaningful some that seemed meaningless. For example, since no universal sentence ("All swans are white") is conclusively verifiable, since it is not possible to know when we have examined all the cases there are, it turns out that no universal sentences—except purely logical ones—are meaningful. But of course many universal sentences are meaningful.

There have been attempts to patch up the criterion, to make it workable. Carl Hempel has suggested translatability-into-an-empiricist-language as a workable criterion. An empiricist language would be roughly the language of the *Principia Mathematica* with only predicates for observable characteristics. This also has its difficulties.[10]

The repeated disappointments the attempt to reformulate the verifiability criterion has been met with have brought about the

---

10. Carl Hempel, "Problems and Changes in the Empiricist Criterion of Meaning," in *Logical Positivism*, ed. by Alfred J. Ayer (New York: Free Pr., 1959).

abandonment of the criterion. Some have seen in the failure of the criterion a failure of empiricism. But many empiricists are content to work with only their intuitive notions of what is meaningful, which after all are what the criterion was supposed to capture.

TRUTH-FUNCTIONALITY

Truth-functionality and extensionality are often treated as one principle, and there is good reason for that; for, given certain plausible assumptions—as that the reference of a sentence is its truth-value—the two principles do seem to be equivalent. Nevertheless it will be easier for us to treat them here as two principles, or at least as two aspects of the same principle. The claim of extensionality is that the truth-value of a sentence is a function of the reference of the expressions that occur in that sentence; the claim of truth-functionality is the more restricted claim that the truth-value of a compound sentence is a function of the truth-values of the sentences it contains.

But although the two principles can be separated, it happens that precisely the same sorts of examples give difficulty to each of them. Belief-sentences are an embarrassment for extensionality; as a matter of fact, the truth-value of belief-sentences is not a function of the truth-value of the sentence contained in them. And no one has succeeded in showing that there is any sort of truth-functional sentence to which belief-sentences are, as a rule, equivalent. Necessity-sentences likewise create a difficulty for both truth-functionality and extensionality. A sentence like

Necessarily, Quine is Quine

is true; but its truth-value is not a function of the truth-value of the contained sentence "Quine is Quine"; if it were, then

Necessarily, my pen is black

would also be true, since "My pen is black" has the same truth-value as "Quine is Quine," namely, truth. But it is false that necessarily my pen is black; it might well have been blue. So, in a statement of necessity, the truth or falsity of the whole is not determined by the truth or falsity of the parts—thus, the difficulty for the principle of truth-functionality.

But extensionality fails as well here. For although the sentence

Necessarily, Quine is Quine

is true; and it is also true that "Quine" and "the author of *Word and Object*" have the same reference; nevertheless, it is false that

Necessarily, Quine is the author of
Word and Object.

He could have neglected to write that book. And so expressions referring to the same thing cannot be substituted one for the other in the context of necessity without changing the truth value of the necessity-sentence.

The conclusion we might draw concerning truth-functionality is similar to a conclusion that was suggested regarding extensionality: The evidence is against the principle, and, there being no reason to hold it in the face of the evidence, we should give it up. That is a negative conclusion, but it has positive ramifications; for if truth-functionality and extensionality are to be abandoned, it follows that the logic that we introduced in the first chapter will have to be supplemented. The system of *Principia Mathematica* is a theory of argument, and every sort of compound proposition is involved in certain unique sorts of valid argument. And if truth-functional compounds are not the only sorts of compounds there are, then there are other sorts of valid arguments; besides arguments involving belief and necessity, which are not reducible to truth-functions, there are valid arguments involving cause, obligation, knowledge and action.[11] The logic of belief, the logic of necessity, and so on, are not reducible to truth-functional logic, or to predicate logic. The general realization that this is so was followed by a rapid development in the investigation of those logics.

The logic of necessity can serve as an example. C. I. Lewis was investigating that logic early in the century, at about the same time the *Principia* was being published;[12] yet there was no great

11. It really makes no difference whether we talk about valid arguments concerning belief, etc., or about valid principles governing those notions; the arguments are not truth-functionally valid, and the principles are not truth-functional tautologies.

12. Lewis's early work on modal logic is surveyed and continued in C. I. Lewis and C. H. Langford, *Symbolic Logic* (New York: Century, 1932).

general interest in the subject until about 1945. Since that time the problems surrounding the logic of necessity—modal logic so-called—have moved into the foreground of philosophic concern, and occupy a good deal of space in the journals.

There is not just one modal logic; the number of modal logics corresponds to the number of different notions of necessity. The most useful and well-known are among those developed originally by Lewis himself. Each of these logics is characterized by a set of axioms and rules of inference, which are meant to be added to the axioms and rules of some system of truth-functional logic (perhaps those of the *Principia*). Let us take as an example the system of logic T, which is not a Lewis system. T consists of axioms and rules for truth-functional logic, plus the following axioms and rule:

A1. If necessarily p, then p.
$(Np \supset p)$

A2. If it is necessary that if p then q,
then if necessarily p then necessarily q.
$(N(p \supset q) \supset (Np \supset Nq))$

Rule of necessitation: If p is a theorem
of this system, then *necessarily p* is also
a theorem.

The first axiom says that whatever is necessarily true is true, which is plausible. The second says that whatever necessarily follows from a necessary proposition is also necessary. The rule enables us to say that any theorem of this system is a necessary truth; since

If p then if q then p
$(p \supset (q \supset p))$,

which is derivable from the truth-functional part of the system is a theorem of the system, so is

Necessarily if p then if q then p
$N(p \supset (q \supset p))$.

The notion of necessity which is characterized by this system T is different from the types of necessity characterized by other systems with different axioms and rules. We may call this notion "necessity$_T$." We might find, in any particular context, that necessity$_T$ is inadequate, that it does not have the logical features required in that context. Necessity$_T$ might be inadequate for a discussion of mathematical necessity; perhaps one of the Lewis systems would be more satisfactory there. That can only be decided by a painstaking comparison of the theorems of T with the characteristics of mathematical necessity. Of course it is entirely possible that there is more than one sort of mathematical necessity, but in any case even after we have settled the problem of mathematical necessity, we are left to decide what system is appropriate to the necessity of the laws of nature. If there are other types of necessity, we must decide for each of those types which system characterizes the necessity involved.

The intensive work that has been done in modal logic has provided some cues for work in epistemic logic, the logic of knowledge. There might, for example, be a concept of knowledge that could be captured by axioms and analogous to the axioms of the modal system T:

A1. If S knows that *p*, then *p*.

A2. If S knows that if *p* then *q*, then if S knows that *p*, then S knows that *q*.

It would be difficult to carry the analogy very far. Jaakko Hintikka has attempted to provide us with an epistemic logic that is related to more complex modal logics.[13] Even when such attempts fail, they are instructive; investigation into the failures will make clear what is and what is not possible in a logic of knowing.

ONTOLOGICAL COMMITMENT

If we had only to admit the existence of individual objects in the universe, then the logic of the *Principia* would probably have been adequate. But it seems that that logic is not adequate; what difference will that make? What sort of relation is there, after all, between the sorts of sentences we take to be true and the sorts of entities we must allow in our universe?

Quine has formulated a way of deciding what sorts of entities we are committed to by the sentences we accept: Where we accept a sentence of the sort "There is an *x* which is such and

13. *See* his *Knowledge and Belief* (Ithaca, N.Y.: Cornell Univ. Pr., 1962).

such," we commit ourselves to the existence of the sort of thing that can be such and such.[14] For example, if we admit the truth of "There is an x which is a black dog" we commit ourselves to the existence of black dogs—not of blackness, nor of doghood, but of concrete, individual, black dogs. The only way we could commit ourselves to the existence of an abstract entity like blackness would be to accept as true such a sentence as "There is an x which is blackness." Presumably we are not required to accept the existence of blackness unless we are somehow *required* to admit the truth of such a sentence. If we could avoid that by translating all sentences about blackness into sentences about black things, we could avoid having to admit the existence of blackness; we would only be committed to there being black things. And in general if all existential sentences ("There is an x such that . . .") could be translated into sentences asserting the existence only of individual objects, then there would be no need for us to admit anything except individual objects into our universe.

Chisholm suggests a similar criterion of commitment: If we know some sentence to be true, and if the truth of that sentence entails the existence of a certain sort of entity, and there is no way of rephrasing that sentence so that it does not entail that sort of entity, then it would be reasonable to suppose that entities of that sort exist.[15] Now one such unrephrasable sentence, as Chisholm points out, is this:

> There is something which is feared by
> Jones and anticipated by Smith.

Such sentences are sometimes known to be true. By Quine's criterion of ontological commitment what such a sentence would commit us to would be something that would be feared and anticipated, namely, a state of affairs. There is no way to rephrase the sentence so that only individual entities are entailed and not states of affairs as well. So, on Quine's criterion, accepting the truth of such statements—statements we called intentional[16] in chapter 4—commits us to the existence of states of affairs.

14. W. V. O. Quine, "On What There Is," in his *From a Logical Point of View* (Cambridge: Harvard Univ. Pr., 1953), p. 12ff.

15. *See* Roderick M. Chisholm's "Problems of Identity," in Milton Munitz, ed., *Identity and Individuation* (New York: New York Univ. Pr., 1971), pp. 3–30.

16. I call the reader's attention to the fact that in this chapter we have encountered two different notions: The inten*t*ional and the inten*s*ional.

There are three clearly defined positions one could take in this matter. If you are determined that states of affairs (and properties and propositions, and other intensional entities) shall remain unwelcome, you will reject the importance of intentional sentences for a description of the world. That is Quine's direction. If you feel that intentional sentences cannot be ignored, that the fact that I believe so and so is as much a fact about the world as that such and such a particle is moving in such and such a direction, you will admit the existence of states of affairs. That is Chisholm's position. But if, like Prior, you want to avoid admitting that there are states of affairs, and you do not want to ignore intentional sentences, you will reject criteria of ontological commitment like those of Quine and Chisholm.[17]

Where does the truth lie? It is difficult to see how intentional sentences can be excluded from consideration, or replaced with pale behavioral accounts. It is difficult too to see how Prior can avoid some sort of commitment based on what we know to be true. If some sentence that I know to be true entails that there are things of a certain sort, then how am I to avoid the conclusion that there are entities of that sort? But the reader is referred to Prior's *Objects of Thought* for a lucid discussion of these matters.

TRUTH

The last topic to be taken up is, appropriately, truth. If there is such a thing as a theory of truth, two theories have dominated the traditional discussion of truth, the correspondence theory and the coherence theory. The first sees truth as a relation between propositions and the world: We speak *truly* when we say of what is *that* it is, according to Aristotle. The correspondence is between what is asserted and what is. The coherence theory, on the other hand, locates truth in the coherence of a proposition with a body of propositions all taken to be true. Both theories talk about propositions and so raise the hackles of those

---

It is important not to confuse them: Psychological sentences are supposed to be intentional; the study of the intension, or sense of an expression is to be distinguished from the study of its extension, or reference.

17. Arthur N. Prior, *Objects of Thought* (Oxford: Clarendon Pr., 1971).

to whom propositions and other intensional entities are distasteful.[18]

Either theory could be reconstrued as being about beliefs; but beliefs, as independently existing entities, are no less distasteful than propositions to the ascetic philosopher who hopes to show that there are only individual objects in the universe. Such a philosopher might welcome a reconstrual of one of these theories in terms of sentences—concrete graphite-on-paper or waves-in-the-ether sentences, but it is not clear that either the correspondence theory or the coherence theory can be construed as being about sentences.

Of the two theories, the coherence theory faces the most obvious difficulties; on that theory all that is required for the truth of a proposition is that it be logically consistent with and supported by a body of propositions all of which are taken to be true. If that is what we believe truth is, we must admit ourselves unable ever to determine whether the belief of another man is true, since it is impossible for us to determine what all of his other beliefs are. The theory must at least be modified to make truth consistency with a *generally accepted* body of propositions, and not just any body of propositions whatever.

But there is a more serious difficulty. There is, to adapt an argument from Chisholm, an intuitively acceptable condition laid down by Tarski for any theory of truth: Whatever theory of truth we accept, it must turn out that "Snow is white" is true if and only if snow is white. That means that snow's being white is a necessary and sufficient condition for the truth of "Snow is white," but, according to the coherence theory, *all* that is necessary for the truth of that sentence is its coherence with some body of propositions, and if that's *all* that's necessary, then snow's being white is *not* necessary to the truth of "Snow is white." This seems to present a difficulty for the coherence theory, and it isn't obvious how Tarski's condition might be denied; it *is* a necessary and sufficient condition for the truth of "Snow is white" that snow is white.

For someone not sympathetic with the coherence theory, it is tempting to suppose that that theory arises out of a confusion. The theory of truth must not be confused with the theory of evidence. The evidence we have for any given proposition is a

18. For a discussion of recent theories of truth, *see* Roderick M. Chisholm's *Theory of Knowledge* (Englewood Cliffs, N.J.: Prentice-Hall, 1966), the last chapter.

matter of coherence of the propositions which support that proposition; any theory of evidence will therefore be a coherence theory. But evidence does not add up to truth. It is possible to have a great deal of evidence for a false proposition. But philosophers have not always been very careful to separate the two notions, evidence and truth; consequently, they have sometimes seemed to mistake what makes a proposition evident for what makes it true. But while evidence lies in coherence, there is not good reason, once we have the two notions distinguished, to suppose that truth lies in coherence.

What is left for us, then, if we would prefer to avoid the correspondence theory with its talk of propositions? We might look into what has been called the "disappearance theory of truth," but is more commonly called the "redundancy theory." In an article "Truth" appearing in *Analysis* in 1949, P. F. Strawson espoused such a theory.[19] The plain theory goes like this: To say "It's true that John is going" is to say no more than "John is going." The longer sentence may be a way of underlining what we have to say, but it does not say any more than the short sentence. To say "It is false that John is going" is simply to say "John is not going." What about sentences like "That's true," or "What he says is true"? The word "true" cannot be simply redundant in those sentences. The answer, according to the theory, is that those sentences are used simply to express agreement with what someone has said—like saying "Right!" And other uses of "true" and "false" are to be analyzed along these lines. All of this goes to show, if it is correct, that there is really no need to talk about propositions and their relation to the world, at least not for the theory of truth. Nowhere in the description of the theory has it been suggested that the theory is required to consider such things as propositions.

Strawson's paper led to what is known as the Strawson-Austin debate, a series of papers by Strawson and J. L. Austin on the nature of truth.[20] The interested reader is referred to the papers themselves; I will try here only to suggest the nature of Austin's criticism. Strawson had argued that we say "It is true that *p*" simply to underline what we are saying; we do not add anything to the message. But Austin accused Strawson of paying attention only to what we do with sentences like "It is true that *p*" and

19. *Analysis* 9 (1949): 83–97.
20. The entire debate is reprinted in *Truth*, ed. by G. W. Pitcher (Englewood Cliffs, N.J.: Prentice-Hall, 1964).

ignoring what we *say* in uttering such sentences. Certainly we could say "It is true that *p*" to underline our belief that *p* but we should not ignore the fact that we do that underlining by making a statement about a relation between the statement *p* and the facts. What we *say* in this case is a statement about a statement—regardless of what we do in saying that. And what we say is that the facts are such as are normally described by making that statement.

CONCLUSION

What is the condition of analytic philosophy at the present time? There is serious doubt about the principles of extensionality and truth-functionality, and with them the conviction that either (1) the structure of *Principia Mathematica* mirrors the structure of the world, or (2) everything that can be meaningfully said can be said in the framework of the *Principia*. Phenomenalism has been put away, as unworkable. Behaviorism can only be considered adequate if we ignore most of the truths about what people do. What is left for analytic philosophy?

If it is difficult to say just what analytic philosophy is, it is not so difficult to point out some of the things that analytic philosophy is not. Analytic philosophy is not extensionality, nor ideal languages, nor phenomenalism, nor behaviorism. The proof is simple. The important objections to all these positions—extensionality, phenomenalism, behaviorism and the others—came not from outside analytic philosophy, but from within. The telling objections to the verifiability criterion came from positivists; atomism was finally repudiated by atomists.

Certainly there are still philosophical behaviorists; some of the most important contemporary philosophers fit that description. But—and this is the point—they are not writing in ignorance of or in contempt of the developments. Quine, for example, calls himself a behaviorist "if anyone is," but he admits Brentano's thesis—that not all statements about mental events can be translated into statements about behavior—and acknowledges that he can hope at best to conform only parts of our body of knowledge to his rigorous standards.

Both his behaviorism and the objection to it have their place in analytic philosophy. However closely that philosophy was identified at first with particular doctrines, it has become clear that it is above all an approach to philosophical problems, whatever their solutions might be. It is characterized by a concern for clarity and a willingness to apply the machinery of logic to the problems of philosophy. What holds analytic philosophers together is a common philosophical language; and it may be that that language is all that distinguishes analytic philosophy from other philosophical traditions that share the concern of the analyst for clarity, and his willingness to use formal tools. I suspect that the reason that analysis can so readily be distinguished from the particular doctrines that analysts have held is that analytic philosophy is, at its best, just good philosophizing, and not in any deep way distinguishable from any other sort of philosophy.

SUGGESTIONS
FOR FURTHER READING

There are two short introductions to the philosophy of logic, W. V. O. Quine's *Philosophy of Logic* (Englewood Cliffs, N.J.: Prentice-Hall, 1970) and Hilary Putnam's book with the same title (New York: Harper, 1971). Unfortunately, both of those books presuppose more background than this chapter has been able to provide. A better way to start would be with an introductory logic text and *The Encyclopedia of Philosophy* (ed. by Paul Edwards [New York: Macmillan, 1967]). Irving Copi's *Introduction to Logic* (New York: Macmillan, the most recent edition), a textbook that has for twenty years been used almost universally in "baby" or beginning logic courses, has a short section on symbolic logic that is not too difficult. For more advanced study, there are many texts available. The *Encyclopedia* articles that will be helpful include the various articles under the "Logic" heading, especially those by Bede Rundle and Arthur N. Prior ("Logical Terms, Glossary of," by B. A. Brody is very helpful); "Referring" and "Synonymity," by Leonard Linsky; "Language, Philosophy of," and "Meaning," by William P. Alston; "Verifiability Principle," by R. W. Ashby; and "Frege, Gottlob," by Michael Dummett. Two logic texts that devote a good deal of space to philosophical problems are Richard Purtill's *Logic for Philosophers* (New York: Harper, 1971), and Karel Lambert and Bas van Fraassen's *Derivation and Counterexample* (Encino, Calif.: Dickenson, 1972).

The important articles include: Gottlob Frege's "On Sense and Denotation," translated from the German by Max Black for

Black and Peter Geach's *Translations from the Philosophical Writings of Gottlob Frege* (Oxford: Blackwell, 1952); Bertrand Russell's "On Denoting," in his *Logic and Knowledge* (London: Allen & Unwin, 1956) in which the theory of descriptions is introduced to meet some of the difficulties Frege was trying to meet with his two-level theory of meaning; W. V. O. Quine's "Reference and Modality," in which Quine shows that the difficulties for substitution that Russell was trying to avoid are also difficulties for quantification, and "On What There Is" are both found in Quine's *From a Logical Point of View* (Cambridge: Harvard Univ. Pr., 1953); Carl G. Hempel's "Problems and Changes in the Empiricist Criterion of Meaning," in Alfred Ayer (ed.) *Logical Positivism* (New York: Free Pr., 1959), in which Hempel reformulates the verifiability criterion; Alfred Tarski's "Semantic Conception of Truth" (*Philosophy and Phenomenological Research* 4 [1944]: 341–75); Roderick M. Chisholm's "Intentionality and the Theory of Signs" (*Philosophical Studies* 3 [1952]: 57); and there are others which can be found in the bibliographies of the *Encyclopedia* articles mentioned. The debate between Austin and Strawson on the nature of truth can be found in many places; for example, in Joseph Margolis (ed.), *Introduction to Philosophical Inquiry* (New York: Knopf, 1968).

The introduction to Bertrand Russell and Alfred North Whitehead's *Principia Mathematica* (Cambridge: Cambridge Univ. Pr., 1910–13) discusses some of these problems; truth-functionality is put forward as a thesis there. Alfred J. Ayer's *Language, Truth, and Logic* (London: Gollancz, 1936) introduced the verifiability criterion to the English-speaking public. Important recent books have been W. V. O. Quine's *Word and Object* (Cambridge, Mass.: Wiley & M.I.T. Pr., 1960), P. F. Strawson's *Introduction to Logical Theory* (New York: Wiley, and London: Methuen, 1952), and Alfred N. Prior's *Objects of Thought* (Oxford: Clarendon Pr., 1971).

BIBLIOGRAPHY OF ANALYTIC PHILOSOPHY

In this bibliography I have attempted to bring together the titles of many of the more important books by analytic philosophers, and of most of the more important anthologies. As for the important articles, some are noted in the "Suggestions for Further Reading" at the end of the chapters of this book; the most recent edition of Edwards and Pap, *A Modern Introduction to Philosophy* (see below) contains detailed and up-to-date critical bibliographies at the end of each section.

The *Philosopher's Index* is a bibliography published quarterly by Bowling Green University. It indexes all English-language philosophy journals, not just those dedicated to analytic philosophy. It includes abstracts of most articles.

Two important reference works are: *The Encyclopedia of Philosophy*, edited by Paul Edwards (New York: Macmillan, 1967); and the Prentice-Hall Foundations of Philosophy series, edited by Monroe and Elizabeth Beardsley. Many of the books in that series are listed below.

The books in part 2 of the bibliography are either important contributions or introductory works; those that are introductory are starred.

ANTHOLOGIES

Ammerman, Robert, ed. *Classics of Analytic Philosophy*. New York: McGraw-Hill, 1965.

Anderson, Alan Ross, ed. *Minds and Machines*. Englewood Cliffs, N.J.: Prentice-Hall, 1964.

Ayer, Alfred J., ed. *Logical Positivism*. New York: Free Pr., 1959.

Bayles, Michael, ed. *Contemporary Utilitarianism*. Garden City, N.Y.: Doubleday, 1968.

Benacerraf, Paul, and Putnam, Hilary, eds. *Philosophy of Mathematics, Selected Readings*. Englewood Cliffs, N.J.: Prentice-Hall, 1964.

Berofsky, Bernard, ed. *Free Will and Determinism*. New York: Harper, 1966.

Binkley, Robert, Bronaugh, Richard, and Marras, Ausonio, eds. *Agent, Action and Reason*. Oxford: Blackwell, 1971.

Black, Max, ed. *Philosophical Analysis*. Ithaca, N.Y.: Cornell Univ. Pr., 1950.

———, ed. *Philosophy in America*. London: Allen & Unwin, 1966.

Borst, C. V., ed. *The Mind-Brain Identity Theory*. London: Macmillan, 1970.

Brandt, Richard B., ed. *Value and Obligation*. New York: Harcourt, 1961.

———, and Nagel, Ernst, eds. *Meaning and Knowledge*. New York: Harcourt, 1965.

Brodbeck, May, and Feigl, Herbert, eds. *Readings in the Philosophy of Science*. New York: Appleton, 1953.

Buck, R. C., and Cohen, Robert, eds. *Boston Studies in the Philosophy of Science: In Memory of Rudolf Carnap*. Vol. 8. Boston: Reidel, 1971.

Butler, A. J., ed. *Analytical Philosophy*. Oxford: Blackwell, 1962.

———, ed. *Analytical Philosophy*. 2d series. Oxford: Blackwell, 1965.

Castañeda, Hector-Neri, ed. *Intentionality, Minds, and Perception*. Detroit: Wayne State Univ. Pr., 1966.

———, and Nakhnikian, G., eds. *Morality and the Language of Conduct*. Detroit: Wayne State Univ. Pr., 1963.

Caton, Charles, ed. *Philosophy and Ordinary Language*. Urbana: Univ. of Illinois Pr., 1963.

Chappell, V. C., ed. *Ordinary Language*. Englewood Cliffs, N.J.: Prentice-Hall, 1964.

———, ed. *Philosophy of Mind*. Englewood Cliffs, N.J.: Prentice-Hall, 1962.

Chisholm, Roderick M., ed. *Realism and the Background of Phenomenology*. Glencoe, Ill.: Free Pr., 1960.

———, and Swartz, Robert J., eds. *Empirical Knowledge: Readings from Contemporary Sources*. Englewood Cliffs, N.J.: Prentice-Hall, 1973.

Danto, Arthur, and Morgenbesser, Sidney, eds. *Philosophy of Science*. New York: Meridian, 1960.

Davidson, Donald, and Hintikka, Jaakko, eds. *Words and Objections: Essays on the Work of W. V. Quine.* Dordrecht: Reidel, 1969.

Donnelly, John, ed. *Logical Analysis and Contemporary Theism.* Bronx, N.Y.: Fordham Univ. Pr., 1972.

Dworkin, Gerald, and Thomson, J. J., eds. *Ethics.* New York: Harper, 1968.

Edel, Abraham, and Krikorian, Y. H., eds. *Contemporary Philosophic Problems.* New York: Macmillan, 1959.

Edwards, Paul, and Pap, Arthur, eds. *A Modern Introduction to Philosophy.* New York: Free Pr., 1973.

Ekman, Rosalind, ed. *Readings in the Problems of Ethics.* New York: Scribner, 1965.

Feigl, Herbert, and Maxwell, Grover, eds. *Current Issues in the Philosophy of Science.* New York: Holt, 1961.

——, and ——, eds. *Minnesota Studies in the Philosophy of Science.* Vol. 3. Minneapolis: Univ. of Minnesota Pr., 1962.

——, and Scriven, Michael, eds. *Minnesota Studies in the Philosophy of Science.* Vol. 1. New York: Appleton, 1953.

——, ——, and Maxwell, Grover, eds. *Minnesota Studies in the Philosophy of Science.* Vol. 2. Minneapolis: Univ. of Minnesota Pr., 1958.

——, and Sellars, Wilfrid S., eds. *Readings in Philosophical Analysis.* New York: Appleton, 1949.

——, Sellars, Wilfrid S., and Lehrer, Keith, eds. *Readings in Philosophical Analysis.* 2d series. New York: Appleton, 1969.

Feyerabend, P. K., and Maxwell, Grover, eds. *Mind, Matter, and Method.* Minneapolis: Univ. of Minnesota Pr., 1966.

Flew, A. G. N., ed. *Body, Mind, and Death.* New York: Macmillan, 1964.

——, ed. *Essays in Conceptual Analysis.* London: Macmillan, 1956.

——, ed. *Logic and Language.* 1st series. Oxford: Blackwell, 1951.

——, ed. *Logic and Language.* 2d series. Oxford: Blackwell, 1953.

Foot, Philippa, ed. *Theories of Ethics.* London: Oxford Univ. Pr., 1967.

Foster, Lawrence, and Swanson, J. W., eds. *Experience and Theory.* Amherst: Univ. of Massachusetts, Pr., 1970.

Griffiths, A. Phillips, ed. *Knowledge and Belief.* Oxford: Oxford Univ. Pr., 1967.

Gustafson, Donald F., ed. *Essays in Philosophical Psychology.* Garden City, N.Y.: Doubleday, 1964.

Hampshire, Stuart, ed. *Philosophy of Mind.* New York: Harper, 1966.

Harris, James, and Severens, Richard, eds. *Analyticity.* Chicago: Quadrangle, 1970.

Henle, Paul, Kallen, H. M., and Langer, Susanne, eds. *Structure, Method, and Meaning: Essays in Honor of H. M. Sheffer.* New York: Liberal Arts, 1951.

Hirst, R. J., ed. *Perception and the External World.* New York: Macmillan, 1965.

Hook, Sidney, ed. *American Philosophers at Work.* New York: Criterion, 1956.

——, ed. *Determinism and Freedom.* New York: New York Univ. Pr., 1958.

——, ed. *Dimensions of Mind.* New York: Colliers, 1961.

Hudson, W. D., ed. *The Is-Ought Question.* New York: St. Martin's, 1969.

Ladd, John, ed. *Ethical Relativism*. Belmont, Calif.: Wadsworth, 1973.

Lehrer, Keith, ed. *Freedom and Determinism*. New York: Random, 1966.

Lewis, H. D., ed. *Contemporary British Philosophy*. 3d series. London: Allen & Unwin, 1956.

Linsky, Leonard, ed. *Semantics and the Philosophy of Language*. Urbana: Univ. of Illinois Pr., 1952.

Loux, Michael, ed. *Universals and Particulars*. New York: Anchor Books, 1970.

Macdonald, M., ed. *Philosophy and Analysis*. Oxford: Blackwell, 1954.

Mace, C. A., ed. *British Philosophy in the Mid-Century*. London: Allen & Unwin, and New York: Macmillan, 1957.

Madden, Edward, ed. *The Structure of Scientific Thought*. Boston: Houghton, 1960.

Margolis, Joseph, ed. *An Introduction to Philosophical Inquiry*. New York: Knopf, 1968.

Marras, Ansonio, ed. *Intentionality, Mind, and Language*. Urbana: Univ. of Illinois Pr., 1972.

Morgenbesser, Sidney M., and White, Morton W., eds. *Philosophy, Science, and Method, Essays in Honor of Ernest Nagel*. New York: St. Martin's, 1969.

Muirhead, J. H., ed. *Contemporary British Philosophy*. 1st series. London: Allen & Unwin 1924.

————, ed. *Contemporary British Philosophy*. 2d series. London: Allen & Unwin, 1925.

Munitz, Milton, ed. *Identity and Individuation*. New York: New York Univ. Pr., 1971.

O'Connor, John, ed. *Modern Materialism*. New York: Harcourt, 1969.

Pears, D. F., ed. *Freedom and the Will*. London: Macmillan, 1963.

————, ed. *The Nature of Metaphysics*. London: Macmillan 1957.

Pitcher, G. W., ed. *Truth*. Englewood Cliffs, N.J.: Prentice-Hall, 1964.

Rescher, Nicholas, ed. *The Logic of Decision and Action*. Pittsburgh: Univ. of Pittsburgh Pr., 1966.

———— et al, eds. *Essays in Honor of Carl G. Hempel*. Dordrecht: Reidel, 1970.

Rorty, Richard, ed. *The Linguistic Turn*. Chicago: Univ. of Chicago Pr., 1967.

Roth, Michael, and Galis, Leon, eds. *Knowing*. New York: Random, 1970.

Schilpp, P. A., ed. *The Philosophy of Alfred North Whitehead*. Evanston, Ill.: Northwestern Univ. Pr., 1941.

————, ed. *The Philosophy of Bertrand Russell*. Evanston, Ill.: Northwestern Univ. Pr., 1944.

————, ed. *The Philosophy of C. D. Broad*. New York: Tudor, 1959.

————, ed. *The Philosophy of C. I. Lewis*. LaSalle, Ill.: Open Court, 1968.

————, ed. *The Philosophy of G. E. Moore*. Evanston, Ill. Northwestern Univ. Pr., 1942.

————, ed. *The Philosophy of Karl Popper*. LaSalle, Ill.: Open Court, 1973.

————, ed. *The Philosophy of Rudolph Carnap*. Evanston, Ill.: Northwestern Univ. Pr., 1963.

Sellars, Wilfrid S., and Hospers, John, eds. *Readings in Ethical Theory*. New York: Appleton, 1970.

Strawson, P. F., ed. *Philosophical Logic*. Oxford: Oxford Univ. Pr., 1967.

Stroll, Avrum, ed. *Epistemology*. New York: Harper, 1967.

Swartz, Robert, ed. *Perceiving, Sensing, and Knowing.* Garden City, N.Y.: Doubleday, 1965.

Taylor, P. W., ed. *The Moral Judgment.* Englewood Cliffs, N.J.: Prentice-Hall, 1963.

Wartofsky, Marx W., ed. *Boston Studies in the Philosophy of Science.* New York: Humanities Pr., 1963.

Weitz, Morris, ed. *Twentieth Century Philosophy: The Analytic Tradition.* New York: Free Pr., 1966.

White, A. R., ed. *The Philosophy of Action.* Oxford: Oxford Univ. Pr., 1968.

Wiener, P. P., ed. *Readings in Philosophy of Science.* New York: Scribner, 1953.

Williams, Bernard, and Montefiore, Alan, eds. *British Analytical Philosophy.* London: Routledge & Kegan Paul, 1965.

BOOKS

*Alston, William P. *Philosophy of Language.* Englewood Cliffs, N.J.: Prentice-Hall, 1964.

Anscombe, G. E. M. *Intention.* Oxford: Blackwell, 1957.

———. *An Introduction to Wittgenstein's Tractatus.* London: Hutchinson, 1959.

———, and Geach, P. T. *Three Philosophers: Aristotle, Aquinas, Frege.* Ithaca, N.Y.: Cornell Univ. Pr., 1961.

Armstrong, D. M. *A Materialist Theory of the Mind.* London: Routledge & Kegan Paul, 1967.

———. *Perception and the Physical World.* London: Routledge & Kegan Paul, 1961.

Aune, Bruce. *Knowledge, Mind, and Nature.* New York: Random, 1967.

Austin, J. L. *How to Do Things with Words.* Oxford: Clarendon Pr., 1962.

———. *Philosophical Papers.* Ed. by G. J. Warnock and J. O. Urmson. Oxford: Clarendon Pr., 1961.

———. *Sense and Sensibilia.* Ed. by G. J. Warnock. Oxford: Clarendon Pr., 1962.

Ayer, Alfred J. *The Concept of a Person.* London: Macmillan, 1963.

———. *Foundations of Empirical Knowledge.* London: Macmillan, 1940.

———. *Language, Truth, and Logic.* London: Gollancz, 1936.

———. *Metaphysics and Common Sense.* San Francisco: Freeman, Cooper, 1970.

———. *Probability and Evidence.* New York: Columbia Univ. Pr., 1972.

———. *The Problem of Knowledge.* London. Macmillan & Penguin, 1956.

———. *Russell and Moore: The Analytical Heritage.* Cambridge: Harvard Univ. Pr., 1971.

*——— et al. *The Revolution in Philosophy.* London: Macmillan, 1956.

Baier, Kurt. *The Moral Point of View.* Ithaca, N.Y.: Cornell Univ. Pr., 1958.

Bergmann, Gustav. *Logic and Reality.* Madison: Univ. of Wisconsin Pr., 1964.

———. *The Metaphysics of Logical Positivism.* London: Longmans, 1954.

———. *Philosophy of Science.* Madison: Univ. of Wisconsin Pr., 1957.

———. *Realism.* Madison: Univ. of Wisconsin Pr., 1967.

Berofsky, Bernard. *Determinism.* Princeton, N.J.: Princeton Univ. Pr., 1971.

Black, Max. *A Companion to Wittgenstein's Tractatus.* Ithaca, N.Y.: Cornell Univ. Pr., 1964.

———, and Geach, Peter. *Translations from the Philosopohical Writings of Gottlob Frege.* Oxford: Blackwell, 1952.

———. *Models and Metaphors.* Ithaca, N.Y.: Cornell Univ. Pr., 1962.

———. *The Nature of Mathematics.* London: Kegan Paul, and New York: Harcourt, 1933.

———. *Problems of Analysis.* London: Routledge & Kegan Paul, 1954.

Braithwaite, R. B. *Scientific Explanation.* Cambridge: Cambridge Univ. Pr., 1953.

*Brandt, Richard B. *Ethical Theory.* Englewood Cliffs, N.J.: Prentice-Hall, 1959.

Broad, C. D. *Mind and Its Place in Nature.* London: Routledge, 1925.

———. *Scientific Thought.* London: Routledge, 1923.

Butrick, Richard. *Carnap on Meaning and Analyticity.* New York: Humanities Pr., 1970.

Carnap, Rudolf. *Formalization of Logic.* Studies in Semantics, vol. 2. Cambridge: Harvard Univ. Pr., 1943.

———. *Foundations of Logic and Mathematics.* Chicago: Univ. of Chicago Pr., 1939.

———. *Introduction to Semantics.* Studies in Semantics, vol. 1. Cambridge: Harvard Univ. Pr., 1942.

———. *The Logical Structure of the World.* Trans. by Rolf George. Berkeley: Univ. of California Pr., 1969. (Originally published in German, 1928.)

———. *The Logical Syntax of Language.* New York: Harcourt, 1937.

———. *Meaning and Necessity.* Chicago: Univ. of Chicago Pr., 1947; 2d ed., 1956.

———. *Philosophical Foundations of Physics.* Ed. by Martin Gardner. New York and London: Basic Books, 1956.

Chihara, Charles. *Ontology and the Vicious Circle Principle.* Ithaca, N.Y.: Cornell Univ. Pr., 1973.

Chisholm, Roderick M. *Human Freedom and the Self.* Lawrence: Univ. of Kansas Pr., 1964.

———. *Perceiving: A Philosophical Study.* Ithaca, N.Y.: Cornell Univ. Pr., 1957.

*———. *Theory of Knowledge.* Englewood Cliffs, N.J.: Prentice-Hall, 1966.

——— et al. *Philosophy.* Englewood Cliffs, N.J.: Prentice-Hall, 1964.

Cornman, James. *Metaphysics, Reference, and Language.* New Haven: Yale Univ. Pr., 1966.

*——— and Lehrer, Keith. *Philosophical Problems and Arguments: An Introduction.* New York: Macmillan, 1968.

Danto, Arthur. *Analytical Philosophy of Action.* Cambridge: Cambridge Univ. Pr., 1973.

———. *Analytical Philosophy of Knowledge.* Cambridge: Cambridge Univ. Pr., 1968.

*———. *What Philosophy Is: A Guide to the Elements.* New York: Harper, 1971.

Dray, William. *Laws and Explanation in History.* Oxford: Oxford Univ. Pr., 1957.

Dretske, Fred. *Seeing and Knowing.* London: Routledge & Kegan Paul, 1969.

Ducasse, C. J. *Nature, Mind, and Death.* LaSalle, Ill.: Open Court, 1951.

———. *Philosophy as a Science.* New York: Oskar Piest, 1941.

Edwards, Paul. *The Logic of Moral Discourse.* New York: Free Pr., 1955.

Feibleman, J. K. *Inside the Great Mirror.* The Hague: Martinus Nijhoff, 1958.

Feigl, Herbert. *The "Mental" and the "Physical."* Minneapolis: Univ. of Minnesota, Pr., 1967.

Flew, Anthony. *Evolutionary Ethics.* New York: St. Martin's, 1968.

———. *God and Philosophy.* New York: Dell, 1969.

Frank, Philipp. *Foundations of Physics.* Chicago: Univ. of Chicago Pr., 1946.

———. *Philosophy of Science.* Englewood Cliffs, N.J.: Prentice-Hall, 1957.

*Frankena, William. *Ethics.* Englewood Cliffs, N.J.: Prentice-Hall, 1963.

Gale, Richard. *The Language of Time.* London: Routledge & Kegan Paul, 1968.

Geach, Peter. *Mental Acts.* London: Routledge & Kegan Paul, 1957.

———. *Reference and Generality.* Ithaca, N.Y.: Cornell Univ. Pr., 1962.

Goldman, A. I. *A Theory of Human Action.* Englewood Cliffs, N.J.: Prentice-Hall, 1970.

Goodman, Nelson. *Fact, Fiction, and Forecast.* Cambridge: Harvard Univ. Pr., 1955.

———. *Language of Art.* Indianapolis: Bobbs-Merrill, 1968.

———. *Problems and Projects.* Indianapolis: Bobbs-Merrill, 1971.

———. *The Structure of Appearance.* Cambridge: Harvard Univ. Pr., 1951.

Hamlyn, D. W. *The Theory of Knowledge.* Garden City, N.Y.: Anchor Books, 1970.

Hampshire, Stuart. *Feeling and Expression.* London: H. K. Lewis, 1961.

———. *Thought and Action.* London: Chatto & Windus, 1959.

Hare, R. M. *Applications of Moral Philosophy.* Berkeley: Univ. of California Pr., 1972.

———. *Essays on Philosophical Method.* Berkeley: Univ. of California Pr., 1971.

———. *Essays on the Moral Concepts.* Berkeley: Univ. of California Pr., 1972.

———. *Freedom and Reason.* Oxford: Clarendon Pr., 1963.

———. *The Language of Morals.* Oxford: Clarendon Pr., 1950.

———. *Practical Inferences.* Berkeley: Univ. of California Pr., 1971.

Harmon, Gilbert. *Thought.* Princeton, N.J.: Princeton Univ. Pr., 1973.

*Harre, R. *The Philosophies of Science.* London: Oxford Univ. Pr., 1972.

Hart, H. L. A. *Punishment and Responsibility.* Oxford: Oxford Univ. Pr., 1968.

Hempel, Carl G. *Aspects of Scientific Explanation.* New York: Free Pr., 1965.

———. *Fundamentals of Concept Formation in Empirical Science.* Chicago: Univ. of Chicago Pr., 1952.

*———. *Philosophy of Natural Science.* Englewood Cliffs, N.J.: Prentice-Hall, 1966.

Hintikka, Jaakko. *Knowledge and Belief.* Ithaca, N.Y.: Cornell Univ. Pr., 1962.

——. *Logic, Language Games, and Information*. Oxford: Oxford Univ. Pr., 1973.

Hospers, John. *Human Conduct*. New York: Harcourt, 1961.

*——. *An Introduction to Philosophical Analysis*. New York: Prentice-Hall, 1953.

——. *Libertarianism*. Los Angeles: Nash, 1971.

*Hudson, W. D. *Modern Moral Philosophy*. Garden City, N.Y. Doubleday, 1970.

Joergensen, Joergen. *The Development of Logical Empiricism*. Chicago: Univ. of Chicago Pr., 1951.

Kenny, Anthony. *Action, Emotion, and Will*. London: Routledge & Kegan Paul, 1963.

Kerner, George. *Revolution in Ethical Theory*. London: Oxford Univ. Pr., 1966.

Kneale, William, and Kneale, Mary. *The Development of Logic*. Oxford: Oxford Univ. Pr., 1962.

Kung, Guido. *Ontology and the Logistic Analysis of Language*. New York: Humanities Pr., 1967.

Ladd, John. *The Structure of a Moral Code*. Cambridge: Harvard Univ. Pr., 1957.

Lazerowitz, Morris. *The Structure of Metaphysics*. London: Routledge & Kegan Paul, 1955.

——. *Studies in Metaphilosophyy*. London: Routledge & Kegan Paul, and New York: Humanities Pr., 1964.

Lean, Martin. *Sense Perception and Matter*. London: Routledge & Kegan Paul, 1953.

Lewis, C. I. *Analysis of Knowledge and Valuation*. LaSalle, Ill.: Open Court, 1947.

——. *Mind and the World Order*. New York: Scribner, 1929.

——. *A Survey of Symbolic Logic*. Berkeley: Univ. of California Pr., 1918.

——. *Values and Imperatives*. Stanford: Stanford Univ. Pr., 1969.

——, and Langford, C. H. *Symbolic Logic*. New York: Century, 1932.

Linsky, Leonard. *Referring*. London: Routledge & Kegan Paul, 1968.

Locke, Don. *Perception and Our Knowledge of the External World*. New York: Humanities Pr., 1967.

Madden, Edward. *Philosophical Problems of Psychology*. New York: Odyssey, 1962.

Malcolm, Norman. *Dreaming*. London: Routledge & Kegan Paul, 1959.

——. *Knowledge and Certainty*. Englewood Cliffs, N.J.: Prentice-Hall, 1963.

——. *Ludwig Wittgenstein: A Memoir*. Oxford: Oxford Univ. Pr., 1958.

Martin, Richard M. *Truth and Denotation*. Chicago: Univ. of Chicago Pr., 1958.

Melden, A. I. *Free Action*. New York: Humanities Pr., 1961.

——. *Rights and Right Conduct*. New York: Humanities Pr., 1959.

Mises, Richard von. *Positivism: A Study in Human Understanding*. Cambridge: Harvard Univ. Pr., 1951.

Moore, G. E. *Ethics*. London: Home Univ. Lib., 1912.

——. *Philosophical Papers*. London: Allen & Unwin, 1959.

——. *Philosophical Studies*. London: Kegan Paul, 1922.

——. *Principia Ethica*. Cambridge: Cambridge Univ. Pr., 1903.

——. *Some Main Problems of Philosophy.* London: Allen & Unwin, 1953.

Morris, C. W. *Foundations of the Theory of Signs.* Chicago: Univ. of Chicago Pr., 1938.

——. *Signs, Language, and Behavior.* New York: Braziller, 1955.

Nagel, Ernest. *Logic without Metaphysics.* Glencoe, Ill.: Free Pr., 1956.

——. *The Structure of Science.* New York: Harcourt, 1961.

Nowell-Smith, P. H. *Ethics.* London: Penguin, 1954.

Ogden, C. K., and Richards, I. A. *The Meaning of Meaning.* London: Kegan Paul, 1923.

Pap, Arthur. *The A Priori in Physical Theory.* New York: King's Crown Pr., 1946.

*——. *Elements of Analytic Philosophy.* Facsimile ed. New York: Hafner, 1972.

*——. *An Introduction to the Philosophy of Science.* Glencoe, Ill.: Free Pr., 1962.

——. *Semantics and Necessary Truth.* New Haven: Yale Univ. Pr., 1958.

Pasch, Alan. *Experience and the Analytic.* Chicago: Univ. of Chicago Pr., 1959.

*Passmore, John. *A Hundred Years of Philosophy.* New York: Basic Books, 1966.

Peters, R. S. *The Concept of Motivation.* London: Routledge & Kegan Paul, 1958.

Plantinga, Alvin. *God and Other Minds.* Ithaca, N.Y.: Cornell Univ. Pr., 1967.

——. *The Nature of Necessity.* Oxford: Oxford Univ. Pr., 1973.

Popper, Karl. *Conjectures and Refutations.* New York: Basic Books, 1962.

——. *The Logic of Scientific Discovery.* London: Hutchinson, 1958. (Originally published in German, 1935.)

——. *Objective Knowledge.* Oxford: Oxford Univ. Pr., 1972.

——. *The Open Society and Its Enemies.* London: Kegan Paul, 1945.

——. *The Poverty of Historicism.* London: Routledge & Kegan Paul, 1957.

Price, H. H. *Belief.* New York: Humanities Pr., 1969.

——. *Hume's Theory of the External World.* Oxford: Clarendon Pr., 1940.

——. *Perception.* London: Methuen, 1932.

Prior, Arthur N. *Formal Logic.* London: Oxford Univ. Pr., 1962.

——. *Objects of Thought.* Oxford: Clarendon Pr., 1971.

——. *Past, Present, and Future.* Oxford: Clarendon Pr., 1967.

——. *Time and Modality.* Oxford: Clarendon Pr., 1957.

——. *Time and Tense.* London: Oxford Univ. Pr., 1968.

*Putnam, Hilary. *Philosophy of Logic.* New York: Harper, 1971.

Quine, W. V. O. *From a Logical Point of View.* Cambridge: Harvard Univ. Pr., 1953.

——. *Methods of Logic.* New York: Holt, 1959.

*——. *Philosophy of Logic.* Englewood Cliffs, N.J.: Prentice-Hall, 1970.

——. *The Roots of Reference.* LaSalle, Ill.: Open Court, 1973.

——. *Word and Object.* Cambridge, Mass.: Wiley & M.I.T. Pr., 1960.

Ramsey, F. P. *The Foundation of Mathematics.* London: Kegan Paul, 1931.

Rawls, John. *A Theory of Justice.* Cambridge: Harvard Univ. Pr., Belknap Pr., 1971.

Reichenbach, Hans. *Experience and Prediction*. Chicago: Univ. of Chicago Pr., 1938.

———. *The Rise of Scientific Philosophy*. Berkeley: Univ. of California Pr., 1951.

Rescher, Nicholas. *The Coherence Theory of Truth*. Oxford: Oxford Univ. Pr., 1970.

———. *Distributive Justice*. Indianapolis: Bobbs-Merrill, 1966.

———. *Essays in Philosophical Analysis*. Pittsburgh: Univ. of Pittsburgh Pr., 1969.

———. *Scientific Explanation*. New York: Free Pr., 1970.

*Rudner, Richard. *Philosophy of Social Science*. Englewood Cliffs, N.J.: Prentice-Hall, 1966.

Russell, Bertrand. *Analysis of Matter*. New York: Harcourt, 1927.

———. *Analysis of Mind*. New York: Macmillan, 1921.

———. *A History of Western Philosophy*. London: Allen & Unwin, and New York: Simon & Schuster, 1946.

———. *Human Knowledge: Its Scope and Limits*. London: Allen & Unwin, and New York: Simon & Schuster, 1948.

———. *An Inquiry into Meaning and Truth*. New York: Norton, 1940.

———. *Introduction to Mathematical Philosophy*. New York and London: Allen & Unwin, 1919.

———. *Logic and Knowledge*. Ed. by R. C. Marsh. London: Allen & Unwin, 1956.

———. *My Philosophical Development*. London: Allen & Unwin, 1959.

———. *Mysticism and Logic and Other Essays*. London: Longmans, 1918.

———. *Our Knowledge of the External World*. London: Allen & Unwin, 1914.

———. *The Principles of Mathematics*. Cambridge: Cambridge Univ. Pr., 1903.

———. *The Problems of Philosophy*. London: Oxford Univ. Pr., and New York: Henry Holt, 1912.

———, and Whitehead, Alfred North. *Principia Mathematica*. Cambridge: Cambridge Univ. Pr., 1910–13.

Ryle, Gilbert. *The Concept of Mind*. New York: Barnes & Noble, 1949.

———. *Dilemmas*. Cambridge: Cambridge Univ. Pr., 1954.

Saydah, Roger. *The Ethical Theory of Clarence Irving Lewis*. Athens: Ohio Univ. Pr., 1969.

Scheffler, Israel. *Anatomy of Inquiry*. New York: Knopf, 1963.

Schlick, Moritz. *The Problems of Ethics*. New York: Dover, 1939.

Searle, John. *Speech Acts*. Cambridge: Cambridge Univ. Pr., 1970.

Sellars, Wilfrid S. *Form and Content in Ethical Theory*. Lawrence: Univ. of Kansas Pr., 1967.

———. *Science and Metaphysics*. London: Routledge & Kegan Paul, and New York: Humanities Pr., 1968.

———. *Science, Perception, and Reality*. London: Routledge & Kegan Paul, 1963.

Sesonke, Alexander. *Value and Obligation*. Berkeley: Univ. of California Pr., 1957.

*Shaffer, Jerome. *Philosophy of Mind*. Englewood Cliffs, N.J.: Prentice-Hall, 1968.

Shoemaker, Sidney. *Self-Knowledge and Self-Identity*. Ithaca, N.Y.: Cornell Univ. Pr., 1963.

Singer, M. G. *Generalization in Ethics*. New York: Russell & Russell, 1971.

Smart, J. J. C. *Between Science and Philosophy*. New York: Random, 1968.

——. *Outline of a System of Utilitarian Ethics*. Melbourne: Melbourne Univ. Pr., 1961.

——. *Philosophy and Scientific Realism*. London: Routledge & Kegan Paul, 1963.

Stevenson, Charles. *Ethics and Language*. New Haven: Yale Univ. Pr., 1943.

——. *Facts and Values*. New Haven: Yale Univ. Pr., 1963.

Stout, G. F. *Mind and Matter*. Cambridge: Cambridge Univ. Pr., 1931.

Strawson, P. F. *Individuals*. London: Methuen, 1959.

——. *Introduction to Logical Theory*. New York: Wiley, & London: Methuen, 1952.

Tarski, Alfred. *Logic, Semantics, Metamathematics*. Oxford: Clarendon Pr., 1956.

Taylor, Charles. *The Explanation of Behaviour*. London: Routledge & Kegan Paul, 1964.

Taylor, Richard. *Action and Purpose*. Englewood Cliffs, N.J.: Prentice-Hall, 1966.

——. *Metaphysics*. Englewood Cliffs, N.J.: Prentice-Hall, 1963.

Toulmin, Stephen E. *An Examination of the Place of Reason in Ethics*. Cambridge: Cambridge Univ. Pr., 1950.

——. *Philosophy of Science*. London: Hutchinson, 1953.

Urmson, J. O. *Philosophical Analysis*. Oxford: Clarendon Pr., 1956.

Waismann, Friedrich. *Principles of Linguistic Philosophy*. Ed. by R. Harre. New York: St. Martin's, 1965.

*Warnock, G. J. *Contemporary Moral Philosophy*. London: Macmillan, 1967.

——. *English Philosophy since 1900*. London: Oxford University, 1958.

——. *The Object of Morality*. London: Methuen, 1971.

Wellman, Carl. *The Language of Ethics*. Cambridge: Harvard Univ. Pr., 1961.

*White, A. R. *The Philosophy of Mind*. New York: Random, 1967.

White, Morton. *Toward Reunion in Philosophy*. Cambridge: Harvard Univ. Pr., 1956.

Wisdom, John. *Logical Constructions*. New York: Random, 1969.

——. *Other Minds*. Oxford: Blackwell, 1952.

——. *Paradox and Discovery*. Oxford: Blackwell, 1965.

——. *Philosophy and Psycho-Analysis*. Oxford: Blackwell, 1953.

——. *Problems of Mind and Matter*. Cambridge: Cambridge Univ. Pr., 1934.

Wittgenstein, Ludwig. *The Blue and Brown Books*. Oxford: Blackwell, 1958.

——. *Philosophical Investigations*. Trans. by G. E. M. Anscombe. Oxford: Blackwell, 1953.

——. *Tractatus Logico-Philosophicus*. Trans. by C. K. Ogden. London: Kegan Paul; New York: Harcourt, 1922; new trans. by D. F. Pears and B. F. McGuinness, with German text, 1961. (Originally published as "Logisch-Philosophische Abhandlung," *Annalen der Naturphilosophie* 14 [1921]: 185–262.)

Wright, Georg Henrik von. *An Essay in Modal Logic*. Amsterdam: North-Holland, 1951.

———. *Explanation and Understanding*. Ithaca, N.Y.: Cornell Univ. Pr., 1971.

———. *Norm and Action*. New York: Humanities Pr., 1963.

———. *A Treatise on Induction and Probability*. London: Routledge & Kegan Paul, 1951.

———. *Varieties of Goodness*. London: Routledge, 1963.

Ziff, Paul. *Semantic Analysis*. Ithaca, N.Y.: Cornell Univ. Pr., 1960.

———. *Understanding Understanding*. Ithaca, N.Y.: Cornell Univ. Pr., 1972.

INDEX